How to Start a Startup

How to Start a Startup

The Silicon Valley Playbook for Entrepreneurs

Tarun Agarwal

PlatoWorks Inc.
San Francisco, CA

Contents

Preface

How to Start a Startup is based on a Stanford University course of the same name taught by Y Combinator, the prestigious startup accelerator behind billion-dollar companies like Dropbox and Airbnb.

This reference book was published independently by ThinkApps, a product development service powering top Silicon Valley startups and innovative enterprise companies.

ThinkApps' mission is to build great products. From our headquarters in San Francisco, we've designed and developed apps used by millions of users and, in the process, become deeply immersed in the world of startups.

When Y Combinator began its "How to Start a Startup" course, we quickly recognized that its lectures captured many of the key learnings from which early-stage founders would benefit.

Using the course material as a starting point, we decided to write the ultimate Silicon Valley playbook for entrepreneurs — a detailed guide to everything you'll need to know in the earliest stages of your company.

In the chapters that follow, you'll learn from 25+ insiders like:

- **Reid Hoffman**, LinkedIn co-founder
- **Dustin Moskovitz**, Facebook co-founder
- **Marc Andreessen and Ben Horowitz**, co-founders of Netscape and Andreessen Horowitz venture capital firm
- **Peter Thiel**, co-founder of PayPal and Founders Fund, early Facebook investor
- **Ben Silbermann**, Pinterest co-founder and CEO

These experts will reveal the secrets to raising money, building products users love, hiring a great team, getting press coverage, attracting customers, scaling up, and more.

Our hope is that *How to Start a Startup* will take the wisdom and energy of Silicon Valley and spread it worldwide, motivating and educating aspiring entrepreneurs and early-stage startup founders around the globe.

ACKNOWLEDGEMENTS

In addition to acknowledging Stanford University and Y Combinator (especially president Sam Altman), we'd like to recognize the tech founders, executives, and investors who served as speakers for the "How to Start a Startup" course. Their lessons are highlighted throughout this book.

Our thanks also go to Katelan Cunningham and Becky Cruze for their substantial roles in bringing this book to life, as well as to Hrvoje Bielen for cover design.

Introduction

"Starting a successful startup is similar to having kids; it's like a button you press and it changes your life irrevocably." ~Paul Graham

As Paul Graham, co-founder of the prestigious Y Combinator startup accelerator, noted in a lecture at Stanford University, starting a successful startup — like having kids — is life-changing.

It's similar to raising children in another way, as well: it's one of the most challenging yet rewarding things you can do.

STARTUPS ARE EATING THE WORLD

Modern life is shaped by products and services conceived and developed by creative people. Where we live, what food and entertainment we consume, and how we learn, work, and travel are all constantly evolving.

In 2011, legendary entrepreneur and investor Marc Andreessen claimed, "Software is eating the world." Today, it might be more accurate to say that *startups* are eating the world.

But before jumping into an in-depth discussion of startups, let's make sure we're all working off the same definition of these businesses.

As defined by Graham, "A startup is a company designed to grow fast."

Disruption and innovation are the driving forces behind these high-growth companies. Naturally, disrupting the status quo and inventing new products and services is hard work with unpredictable outcomes.

Yet, despite the challenges, there are always entrepreneurs willing to cast off the safe and familiar in order to explore the next frontier.

A large portion of these entrepreneurs seem to be living and working in Silicon Valley. Why is that? And is it necessary for success?

SILICON VALLEY IS STARTUP CENTRAL

Clusters are an important organizing principle. Within the United States, for example, there are clusters of financial firms (Wall Street), automobile makers (Detroit), institutions of higher education (Boston), and entertainment companies (Los Angeles).

With proximity comes dissemination of knowledge, cross-pollination of ideas, and economic efficiency of activities.

As one of the oldest and most successful technology startup clusters, Silicon Valley continues to offer advantages for new entrepreneurs. One can learn from experienced founders, hire talent, find partners, raise funding, etc. more easily than in most places.

However, modern technology companies are unique in that geographic location fundamentally plays a limited role in the final product. Software can increasingly be *built* anywhere and *used* anywhere regardless of where it is built.

EXPORTING SILICON VALLEY EXPERTISE AROUND THE GLOBE

Successful startups are built on new ideas. However, that doesn't mean they have nothing to learn from those that came before. In fact, quite the opposite.

Although the path traveled by each startup will have its own particular twists and turns, there are many common challenges founders will face along the way:

- How can you test the merits of your business idea?
- How do you build the right team to help you?
- How do you raise funding to fuel the engine?
- What legal and financial basics do you need to know?

- How do you get the attention of the market and learn about your (potential) users?

- What's the best way to build and ship products?

- How do you transition from the early stages to realizing a full business?

While each situation is distinct, knowing what has succeeded or failed in similar contexts in the past provides a great starting point.

Fortunately, Silicon Valley has a strong culture of openness, with founders and investors willing to pull back the curtain and share what they've learned along the way. And these lessons will most likely be relevant regardless of where your startup is based.

OUR GOAL

This book brings together advice from more than 25 experienced entrepreneurs, technologists, investors, and business executives behind successful companies of the past and present like Netscape, PayPal, Facebook, LinkedIn, and Pinterest.

Our objective is to share insight across the entire startup journey, from the earliest days when an idea is germinating all the way to when you ship products and begin scaling your business.

You can read this book over a weekend and get the inside

scoop on the hard lessons these smart people have learned over the course of decades.

Ultimately there is no exact recipe for success, but learning from the experience of others can help you to be better prepared as you set off on your own journey to explore the next frontier.

PART I

Early Days

Whether you're working from your living room, a coffee shop, or a coworking space, it's never too early to lay a solid foundation for your business.

1

Read This Before You Even Think About Starting a Startup

Featuring: Sam Altman and Dustin Moskovitz

Becoming an entrepreneur is not all luck and a few late nights. No matter how fun big startup offices look, getting there takes a lot of work.

That was the theme when Sam Altman (president of Y Combinator) and Dustin Moskovitz (co-founder of Facebook and Asana) gave a joint lecture at Stanford University.

THE TRUTH ABOUT STARTUPS

Their talk kicked off with the words of Phil Libin, CEO of Evernote:

> *"People have this vision of being the CEO of a company they started and being on top of the pyramid. Some people are motivated by that, but that's not at all what it's like. What it's really like: Everyone else is your boss – all of your employees, customers, partners, users, [and the] media are your boss. I've never had more bosses and needed to account for more people. If you want to exercise power and authority over people, join the military or go into politics. Don't be an entrepreneur."*

In other words, only start a startup if you feel compelled by a problem and think that building a company will solve it.

Altman said that the passion comes first and the startup second. Along with the passion, you need the aptitude.

Moskovitz broke it down like this:

- **Passion means you need to do it.** You'll need that passion to endure The Struggle and to recruit effectively.

- **Aptitude means the world needs you to do it.** The world needs you somewhere, find where.

ROADMAP TO STARTUP SUCCESS

Got the passion and the aptitude? Then starting a startup may be your true calling. But, you'll need some guidelines to help you flourish.

According to Altman, the first two things you need to maximize startup success are:

1. **A great idea**
2. **A great product**

FINDING YOUR GREAT IDEA

Altman said that no matter how well you execute it, a bad idea will get you nowhere.

This is where a lot of founders drop the ball. There's this pervasive rhetoric in startup culture that it's feasible to start your business with a bad idea. That maybe, if you pivot enough, it'll all work out in the end. But Altman said this is not a good move because it doesn't actually work out.

If your startup succeeds, chances are you'll be working on it for 10 years — if it fails, the timeline is more like five years. If you're going to be in it to see your idea through to success, it's essential that you seriously mull it over and nail down your mission.

The best companies are mission-oriented. With a solid mission in place, you'll get a more motivated team that will rally around you.

HOW DO YOU KNOW IF YOU HAVE A GREAT IDEA?

- **You can answer the question: Why now?** Why is this

the perfect time for this particular idea instead of two years ago or two years from now?

- **You're building something you yourself need.** (If not, get really close to your customers.)

BUILDING A GREAT PRODUCT

After the idea stage, the next step is building an amazing product.

Altman said that looking at market growth is key. You need a market that's going to evolve in 10 years. And it's better to have a small but rapidly growing market, instead of a large but slowly growing market.

Build something that a small number of users love, not just like. If customers are pretty desperate for a solution, then they'll settle on the first product even if it's subpar. If your customers love your product, your startup will grow by word of mouth.

When it comes to getting feedback, handpick your early users. Pinterest co-founder Ben Silbermann (who is featured in a later chapter) actually went up to people in coffee shops and asked them to test the then-unknown social network.

He would even go into the Apple Store and put it in the browsers on all the laptops so it was the first thing customers saw. Whatever works!

THE PRODUCT BUILDING CYCLE

1. **Show it to users.**
2. **Get user feedback.** What do they like? What features would they pay for? Would they recommend it? Would they be bummed if your product went away?
3. **Make a product decision based on your findings.**
4. **Repeat.**

BECOMING A STARTUP FOUNDER IS NOT FOR EVERYONE

If, after reading this, you realize that the startup life isn't for you, that's okay. You've been spared a ton of stress and soul-crushing responsibility. It's not the end of the road for you.

It may not seem like it because of the way the media romanticizes entrepreneurship, but there are other things you can do with your life if you want to maximize your earning potential, have a flexible schedule, and be successful.

When you consider that the 100th engineer at Facebook made far more money than 99% of Silicon Valley entrepreneurs, not being the person in charge starts to look pretty good.

Moskovitz recommended proposing a late-stage feature to an established company if you want to be innovative, use your talent, and receive a big financial return. All of that comes without the stress and responsibility of being the founder because you're not starting from scratch.

Indeed, innovating for a later-stage company means you get access to a massive user base, existing infrastructure, and an established team.

Need more motivation? Google's 1,500th employee created Google Maps. Facebook's 250th hire led the project for the "Like" button.

THE TAKE-AWAY

Being an entrepreneur is not the only path to innovative success. But if it is the path for you, read on for insights from some of the top founders, executives, and investors in Silicon Valley.

2

Never Stop Learning

Featuring: Paul Graham

At the end of the day, founding a startup primarily requires you to do one thing: learn.

According to Paul Graham, co-founder of Y Combinator, learning should be one of your main priorities as a founder.

His advice seems simple enough, but starting a startup is actually a lot more counterintuitive than it seems. You can't just trust your intuition.

He compared entrepreneurship to skiing. Your instinct is to lean back. But if you do, you'll fly down the hill out of control. You have to suppress those instincts. You have to keep a list in your head of what to do and not to do (alternate feet, do not drag inside foot, etc.).

Startups are as unnatural as learning how to ski, and there's a list of counterintuitive things you have to remember in order to keep your business from flying down the hill.

WORK WITH PEOPLE WHO SEEM LIKEABLE

Graham explained that following your instincts can lead you astray. You can, however, trust your instincts when it comes to dealing with people.

Startup founders often don't do this. People may seem charismatic and impressive, but that shouldn't trump your friend test. A good team is a happy team; so hire people who are qualified, but also seem likeable.

UNDERSTAND YOUR USERS

What you need to succeed is not expertise about startups but expertise about *your users*.

Graham said that Mark Zuckerberg did not succeed because he was an expert in startups — after all, Facebook's original formation was an LLC in Florida rather than a C corporation in Delaware (which, as you'll learn in the next chapter, is the standard in the United States). Instead, he succeeded because he understood his users.

It may actually be dangerous to know too much about starting a startup because it could cause you to get ahead of yourself and make generic decisions rather than ones based on your specific business.

Graham explained that too many people think it's as simple as: come up with a great idea, get some investors, hire your friends, and rent office space in SOMA (a neighborhood in San Francisco). But then they realize they may have created a product that people don't actually want.

It's otherwise known as "playing house," and Graham said it's what founders have been trained to do until now.

That's why, even before funding, you need to give users something they love, so you can prove that your idea works and that there's a demand for it.

DON'T LOOK FOR TRICKS

The fact is, there are no shortcuts in starting a startup. There's no master trick to get people to like your product. You just have to make a good product because that's all your users care about.

Graham did concede that faking can sometimes work with investors. But he explained that, even if you're able to fool them a few times, it's ultimately not in your best interest.

So don't get distracted with finding tricks and instead focus on the product.

THERE'S NO RUSH

Startups are all-consuming. It never gets easier, the nature of the problems just changes.

Graham compared the experience to having kids: while it's the best thing in the world, there are a lot of things that are easier to do before you have kids than after.

People seem to think they should start startups in college, but then you have to think about what happens when you're not a student anymore. He said if the ultimate goal is to have a good life, then there's no need to rush.

There are things you can do in your twenties, for example, that you can't do after you've started a startup. Major success actually takes away some of that serendipity that you can't create on your own and you can't get back.

TURN YOUR BRAIN OFF

The perfect startup idea may come to you during a brainstorm or while you're in the shower. Who knows? But Graham suggested that turning your brain off is the best way to get some great startup ideas flowing.

He said that the very best ideas have to start as side projects because they're always such outliers that your conscious mind would reject them as actual companies.

So, how do you do this?

- Learn a lot about things that matter.

- Work on problems that interest you.

- Work with people you like and respect (which will also help you find co-founders).

SOLVE REAL PROBLEMS

Graham said that solving real problems — big or small — is how you'll make a standout product. That product is the driving force behind your startup and in that way, it can be seen as a sort of trial-by-fire system.

He said that the best startups tend to come from true entrepreneurship, not learned entrepreneurship, and it's all rooted in domain expertise.

Larry Page, for example, was genuinely interested in search, not because he thought it would amount to anything but because he wanted to learn. And then it became a little company called Google.

THE TAKE-AWAY

In all of his advice, Graham stayed away from setting any hard and fast rules about starting a startup because it really is a unique journey for every company. You just have to make sure you're staying open-minded and looking for learning opportunities everywhere.

3

Legal and Accounting 101

Featuring: Carolynn Levy and Kirsty Nathoo

Set yourself up with the proper documents and processes now, and you'll save yourself a lot of headaches in the future.

It's definitely one of the less glamorous parts of starting a startup, but filling out the right forms and setting up the right systems goes a long way toward securing investors while protecting yourself and your business.

In a lecture at Stanford University, Carolynn Levy and Kirsty Nathoo — Y Combinator's very own legal and accounting pros — shared all you need to know to make sure you're keeping things legal and official on the back-end, so you can succeed on the front-end.

(Note: This advice is primarily directed towards startups founded in the United States. But the chapter also covers topics like equity allocation and fundraising that will be useful to entrepreneurs around the world.)

FORMATION

The legal formation of your business seems like an obvious step, but just make sure that it's not overlooked. You have to start your company as a separate legal entity to protect yourself from personal liability and ensure that all of the money you make belongs to the company.

But how and where do you go about forming this corporation, which is recommended above other business types like LLCs? While you can pick any state, Levy said that your best option is Delaware.

"Delaware is in the business of forming corporations," she explained. "The law there is very clear and very settled. It's the standard." Bonus, investors are also most comfortable with it.

SETTING UP A DELAWARE CORPORATION

It all starts with a fax telling Delaware that you're creating a company. Then, Nathoo said, "You need to complete a set of documents that approve the by-laws of the company."

These documents create a Board of Directors by assigning officers of the company. Delaware requires that someone has the titles of CEO, President, and Secretary.

You also need to complete documents noting any inventions or code that you as an individual have created so that you can make clear that the company has ownership. Keep in mind the difference between doing something as an individual and doing it on behalf of the company.

GETTING INCORPORATED

You can use a law firm to get incorporated, but a lot of the Y Combinator companies use Clerky — an online service that provides all the documents you need to get going with your business.

Also, Nathoo emphasized again and again the importance of keeping your documents in a safe place because chances are, if an occasion pops up where you need them, you're going to want them ASAP to give to a lawyer or an investor.

EQUITY ALLOCATION

When considering equity allocation, Levy said, "Execution has way more value than the idea." While ideas are important, no one's going to buy one.

> *"Value is created when the whole founder team works together to execute on an idea. You need to resist the urge to give a disproportionate amount of stock to the founder who is credited with coming up with the idea for the company."*

Going with the rule of thumb on allocation at Y Combinator, Levy added, "Stock allocation doesn't have to be exactly equal, but if it's very disproportionate, that's a huge red flag for us."

To investors, it can make your company seem flighty, dishonest, or even self-indulgent. All in all, it just looks like your founders are not in sync with each other.

Levy said this can all be clarified by looking forward and acknowledging among the founding team that everything that happened before the formation of the company shouldn't matter.

Regardless of whose idea it was, who coded it, or who designed it, from the day you formed the company that's ground zero. Onwards and upwards, as they say.

BUYING STOCK (YES, IN YOUR OWN COMPANY)

No matter how many late nights you spend at the office, you don't have stock in your company until you actually buy stock in your company.

You have to sign some papers to make your stock official. It's called a Stock Purchase Agreement and lets you buy part of the company as an individual. You can either pay in cash, IP, invention, or code, so that the company basically owns what you as an individual have contributed to the startup so far.

"We also refer to that stock as being restricted because it vests over time," explained Nathoo.

Since it's restricted and vesting, you need a super-duper important form called the 83(b) Election. Without that form and confirmation that you've signed that form, your and the company's taxes are at stake, as well as any future deals with investors.

VESTING

In case you didn't know, vesting means you get full ownership of your stock over a set period of time. This means that, if you leave before you've built up that amount of time at the company, then the company can repurchase those shares from you at the same price you paid for them.

In Silicon Valley, the standard vesting schedule is four years.

WHY WOULD YOU VEST?

If a founder leaves without vesting, a big part of the equity ownership is in flux, leaving the other founders up a creek.

But Levy said it's also because of "the idea that founders need to be incentivized to keep working on their startup." She added, "If the founder can walk away with his or her full ownership at any point and time, then why would [they] stay and grind away?"

This applies to solo founders, too, as it's a way to show

investors and employees their commitment. Levy said it's a culture point that sets the right tone for the company.

RAISING MONEY

There are two types of rounds in which to raise money: Priced and Non-Priced. These terms mean that either the price (the valuation of the company) is set or it isn't.

Generally, if someone is in what's called a "seed round," the price has not been set. But if they are in Series A or Series B, then the price has been set.

(To learn more about each of these rounds and get advice on how to pitch investors, see Part V on fundraising.)

"Not setting the price is the most straightforward, fast route to getting money," said Nathoo. "This is done through convertible notes or safes."

There's a piece of paper that says the investor is paying an amount now and in return will get stocks at a future date when the price is set by investors in a priced round.

Until then, they're not a shareholder, which means they don't have voting rights. But, these seed investors do want some perks for their risky startup investment.

What are the perks? When the startup goes into priced rounds, the seed investor has the opportunity to buy stocks at a lower price than other investors.

FUTURE DILUTION

Nathoo said to keep in mind how much of your company you're giving away so you don't lose the reins once you hit the priced rounds.

> *"Remember that some money on a low valuation cap is infinitely better than no money at all. And if those are the terms that you can get, then take that money. But it's just something to be aware of and to follow through the whole process so that you can see where this is going to lead you down the road."*

Also, Nathoo said that family and friend investments of a few thousand dollars here or there usually end up causing the most trouble in the future because family and friends aren't familiar with the long-term process.

To avoid this, Nathoo said that investors should be accredited, which means "they have enough money to be able to invest [and] they understand that investing in startups is a risky business."

KNOW THE INVESTOR TERMS

BOARD SEAT

If an investor wants to be on your Board of Directors, that means she wants to keep tabs on how her money is being spent and/or she wants to give advice on your business, whether you want it or not.

Levy said if this request comes up, most often it's best to say no. "Otherwise make sure it's a person who is really going to add value," she said.

ADVISERS

If an investor has given you money, Levy said they should be a de facto adviser. You shouldn't be offering up anything extra for their advice. A good investor will want to help you succeed without any extra benefits or incentives.

PRO-RATA RIGHTS

Levy said that pro-rata rights give you the "right to maintain your percentage ownership in a company by buying more shares in the company in the future." They're a way to prevent losing ownership each time the company sells stock to investors. Make sure you know how these work.

INFORMATION RIGHTS

Sending investors periodic updates is good, but it's a red flag when investors want weekly updates or frequent budget breakdowns.

COMPANY EXPENSES

This is where that divide between personal and company needs to be re-emphasized.

As Nathoo put it, "If you were working at Google, you would not use a Google credit card to buy a toothbrush and toothpaste." Investors have trusted you with a big sum of money to help the company succeed, not to buy your weekly groceries.

She said that, admittedly, this line can get fuzzy in the beginning when you're working from your apartment 24/7.

But a good rule of thumb is to think, if you had to give a line-by-line breakdown to an investor of your expenses, would you be embarrassed by any of them? If so, it's probably not a business expense.

EMPLOYMENT

FOUNDER EMPLOYMENT

As a founder, you should get paid and you should file your payroll taxes. Period.

Besides just basic logistics, Levy said it's important to pay founders because, in the case of a breakup, unpaid wages are a way for the founder that's being fired to use those unpaid hours as leverage to get something else that they want and aren't entitled to — like vesting acceleration.

If they get over on this deal, explained Levy, you not only have a disgruntled ex-employee owning shares of the company, but the rest of the company is now kind of working for them. It's a nasty feeling.

Also, setting up a payroll service is something worth dishing out cash for. But she advises that, when it comes to paying employees at the beginning, stay lean with minimum wage if possible.

HIRING EMPLOYEES

When thinking about the proper paperwork for your employees, first consider if they're an actual employee or a contractor.

Contractor

They sign an IP assignment agreement. They set their own hours, location, and project goals, and they use their own equipment. They sign a consulting agreement, and the company doesn't pay taxes on their behalf. At the end of the year, they get a 1099.

Employee

They also sign an IP assignment agreement, but the company withholds taxes and the employee receives a W2. Your employees also need to have worker's compensation insurance, and you need to ensure that the person has authorization to work in the U.S.

Nathoo suggested services like ZenPayroll to help you take care of those details.

FIRING EMPLOYEES

As you might expect, this is where things can get messy. Still, Levy said this may be one of the first things you do for your startup to prove that you're in it for the long haul. It can mean doing what's right for the company instead of what's easy.

Levy advised some simple steps to make sure it's done quickly and professionally:

1. **Fire quickly.** Nothing good can come of keeping a bad employee on account of procrastination. You'll only lose company culture and maybe even business.

2. **Communicate effectively.** Don't apologize or over-explain. Cut right to the chase, ideally with a third party present.

3. **Pay all wages and accrued vacation right away.** It's the law. That's all there is to it.

4. **Cut off physical and digital access.** Do this as soon as the person is gone.

5. **Repurchase shares.** This, too, should be done right away to further cut all ties with the terminated employee.

THE TAKE-AWAY

Complete all of the proper paperwork up front and keep it in a safe place to avoid crazy legal battles or losing an investor in the future on account of disorganization.

With all of your ducks in a row, you'll be able to make

full use of the insights from this book and rest assured that you're keeping things legal.

PART II

Leadership

To advance your startup to the next stage, you and your co-founders have to learn how to lead.

4

How to Be a Great Founder

Featuring: Reid Hoffman

Entrepreneurial superpowers aren't real. To be a great founder, you need insight — not a cape.

Reid Hoffman may not be on your top 10 list of the most popular founders ever and that's because the story of LinkedIn wasn't a viral one. It wasn't bright, flashy, or famous either.

Unlike the success of Mark Zuckerberg (Facebook), Steve Jobs (Apple), and Jeff Bezos (Amazon), Hoffman and his co-founders at LinkedIn had a less publicized journey of building their audience.

In his talk at Stanford, Hoffman summarized some of what he's learned in becoming a good founder and building the iconic professional network.

Hoffman is the first to say that being an entrepreneur doesn't require superpowers. Patience, perseverance, courage … sure all of those, but no Peter Parker–type abilities.

> *"Competitive differentiation and competitive edge is super important, but it's not actually a function of genius."*

Instead, he said you have to set yourself up for success with the end goal of creating a company that your audience is happy to buy from and your team is happy to work for.

GO FOR CO-FOUNDERS

Hoffman is not just a founder. He's an investor, and he explained that, when he's looking for companies to invest in, he leans toward those with two or three founders.

The way he broke it down makes sense. It may go against your "I got this" entrepreneurial attitude that makes you think you can do it all, but just think about the logistics.

With two or three founders instead of just yourself, your set of skills is inherently more broad. Hoffman points out that with more than one founder, you can compensate for each other's weaknesses and attack a wider set of problems.

Rather than letting your inner superhero sneak in, it may be best to tap a team that you can trust to help you take on all that you want to accomplish with your new venture.

Just try to avoid picking a team that will lead to a "messy divorce," as Hoffman called it. He said that those are usually fatal.

LOCATION, LOCATION, LOCATION

Not all big ideas are meant to grow and thrive in Silicon Valley. Just like the film industry is spreading beyond Hollywood, the entire tech industry doesn't need to take root in the Bay Area.

As a founder, rather than defaulting to one of the world's tech capitals, think about a location that's best for your business. Hoffman explained, "What great founders do is seek the networks that will be essential to their task."

He used the example of Groupon, which is run out of Chicago:

"I don't think Groupon could have ever been founded [in Silicon Valley] … even though it's a software product. One of the things that was central for Groupon for its early days was having massive sales forces. Silicon Valley tends to be pretty adverse to plans that involve [renting] a 25-story building, and in 20 of those stories [having] floors of sales people."

"That kind of plan here tends to not get a lot of interest …

And so it's actually not a surprise that, in fact, Groupon was required to be in Chicago, which is really good at [that]."

When selecting a location, rather than looking for trends in the tech blogs, get specific and narrow regarding your type of business. Think about the trends in investors, workflow, hiring, and organization, and then consider where your model would flourish.

QUITE CONTRARY

There's this idea that you have to be a contrarian in all areas in order to be a true trailblazer, but Hoffman said that's not the case.

Well, it's not exactly the case. In general, Hoffman said, "It's good to be contrarian." After all, it's what helped him push his idea for LinkedIn.

After asking all of the smart people he knew about his idea, he said, "I thought a lot about what ... I know that other people don't know."

For example, most people thought that his idea for LinkedIn was nuts because it was a network product — meaning it wouldn't be valuable until it had at least 500,000 to a million people using it.

Here's Hoffman's rebuttal: "What I knew that the critics didn't know was that I could think of sets of interests in a different way by which people would say ... 'I think a product like this should exist.' And I could level those sets of interest to grow the network to get to enough size that [I] could begin to deliver on the value propositions which Linkedin had."

But this is a very specific example. Hoffman said, "Entrepreneurs are usually given contradicting advice, so it's a matter of knowing when to take certain advice and when to take other advice."

Here are some of those contradictions and which side Hoffman suggests you take, always keeping this nugget of advice in mind: "Part of what makes a great founder is the ability to be flexible across these lines."

TAKE RISKS OR MINIMIZE RISKS?

Keeping it short and sweet, Hoffman said, "You have to be a risk taker."

At the same time, they have to be smart risks, and you have to go into them cautiously and aware. You have to ask yourself, "How do I take a really coherent risk?"

In his presentation, he put up an image of a mouse wearing a helmet, about to go for the cheese on a trap. He then said, "How do I essentially take this risk in an intelligent way that doesn't just go, 'Who cares? Let's go.'?"

GO WITH YOUR VISION OR THE DATA?

Hoffman explained, "Data only exists in the framework of a

vision that you are building. [It's] a hypothesis of where you are moving to."

Sometimes your vision will change as a result of what you learn, but you have to stay focused on information that's aligned with your vision. Numbers can be distracting enough without bringing extraneous ones into the picture.

DO THE WORK OR DELEGATE?

Unfortunately there's no clear line here. You just have to learn when it's good to delegate and when it isn't, but you'll have to do both.

Hoffman added, "In fact, not only do you need to do both, you need to sometimes do one at 100% and … the other at 100%," even if the math doesn't quite add up.

FOCUS ON THE LONG-TERM OR THE SHORT-TERM?

Again, the answer here is both, but don't let that overwhelm you.

"You should always have a long-term vision in mind because if you … completely lose your direction, eventually you will find yourself somewhere in a field and that's not a good path," said Hoffman. "But if you are not focused on solving the problem that's immediately in front of you — you're hosed."

A good exercise could be to go through your daily and weekly to-dos and determine where (if at all) they fall on your path toward your long-term goals.

STAY FIRM IN YOUR IDEA OR PIVOT?

This is a biggie, and not one to be taken lightly. Hoffman said,

> *"Part of what being a great founder is, is being both able to hold the belief — to think about what it is you want to be doing and [where you] want to be going — but also be smart enough that you are essentially listening to criticism, negative feedback, [and] competitive entries."*

Hoffman pointed out that a big part of what will guide you through this and other tough forks in the road is your investment thesis. Constantly keep an eye on your place in the market and your value to it.

If that starts to shift, it could mean that you're losing your product-market fit or that you're finding one. It's all a practice in knowing which.

SO, ARE YOU A GREAT FOUNDER?

After all of this, you may be asking yourself, "Am I a great founder?"

Take note that good founders aren't all cut from the same cloth, which is great because "[t]here are different kinds of entrepreneurial companies [and] there are different problems they're trying to solve," said Hoffman.

"There is not one skill set," he added. "There's an ability to constantly have a vision that's driving you but to [keep] taking input from all sources and then to be creating networks all around you."

THE TAKE-AWAY

One of the most important parts of being a great founder is knowing whether or not you're on the right track. Not the generic track from the old adage, but your own "right track" — your investment thesis.

Staying on that track takes a combination of all the skills mentioned above. And it even means occasionally "crossing uneven ground," as Hoffman put it.

5

Operational Insight: How to Build a Company That Can Manage Itself

Featuring: Keith Rabois

In some ways, building your product is the easy part. Building a company to support your product is when the real leadership starts.

Keith Rabois has learned a lot from serving as an executive at successful tech companies like PayPal, LinkedIn, and Square.

In his lecture at Stanford University, it was clear that seemingly insignificant details like what to feed your employees can have a huge impact on the culture and productivity of your business.

Rabois said "forging a company is a lot harder than forging a product," which is why it's really important that you have some guidelines in place.

And it's more than managing a team and a workflow; it's building a company that will manage itself. He quoted Warren Buffett as saying: **"Build a company that idiots could run because eventually they will."**

But, before the idiots take over, here's how to set up your company to run itself the right way.

YOUR GOAL AS A FOUNDER

Think of your business as an engine.

"At first you have a drawing on a white board and you are architecting it, and it looks especially clean, beautiful, and pretty. But when you actually start translating it to practice, it actually starts looking more [rough] and you're holding it together with duct tape," said Rabois.

Just holding it together takes a lot of effort, and getting it to look like polished metal will take even more. "You want to construct a very high-performance machine," said Rabois. "A machine that almost nobody really has to worry about."

As the leader, he said it's your job to maximize output and

keep your focus there instead of on the input. Only measure your progress.

Most of the time, especially in the beginning, it's going to feel like madness because it probably is. Rabois said that's not only normal, it's good.

> *"If you have too much process, too much predictability, you are probably not innovating fast enough and creatively enough ... It should feel like every day there is a new problem and what you are doing is fundamentally triaging."*

To keep with the medical analogy, he said it's the difference between knowing which problems are fatal and which ones aren't. To have enough perspective and distance to do that, you have to make sure that you're editing, not writing.

BE AN EDITOR

If you'll allow a metaphor switch, Rabois said that all startup teams can be broken down into writers and editors, although not so literally.

You basically have people starting the work from scratch (the "writers"), who then send it up the chain of command to the editors. As a founder, you should definitely be an editor.

This doesn't mean you have to wield a red pen, but it does mean that you have to have some processes in place to make sure your output is intelligent, clear, and consistent.

1. SIMPLIFY

It's a matter of eliminating the extraneous. From workflows to organization methods, it's important that you develop an eye for keeping things lean and efficient by way of elimination.

Rabois said, "It's something you have to practice, but when you get good at it, [with] every step you eliminate … you can improve performance by 30-50%."

"People cannot understand and keep track of long, complicated sets of initiatives," he added. "So you have to distill it down to one, two, or three things and use a framework they can repeat without thinking about."

2. CLARIFY

Think outside your bubble and find ambiguities. Ask lots of questions, big and small. "Did you mean to use this term here?" or "Is this on brand?"

This doesn't mean diluting your message, though. In fact, quite the opposite. Keep in mind some of the most concise copy can be the most powerful, like Apple's "Think Different" slogan.

"You can change the world in 140 characters," Rabois said. "You can build the most important companies in history with a very simple-to-describe concept."

3. ALLOCATE RESOURCES

You can allocate resources in one of two ways: from the top down or from the bottom up. Rabois said that from the bottom up is ideal.

When employees come up with their own initiatives, they're more passionate about them. Not to mention, they're being more resourceful and hopefully eliminating some work for you.

As you begin to do more and more of this, you should be using less and less of that "red ink" each day, and that's how you measure your success.

4. ENSURE CONSISTENT VOICE

In every place your company exists, it should look, sound, and feel like it's coming from the same person.

This means first establishing that voice and making sure that it's understood throughout your team. Then, with this voice in place, your output will be even stronger, more focused, and more determined.

5. DELEGATE

Keep in mind that, within the writer/editor framework, writers do most of the work. So as a founder, you should stay in the editor role. Delegate and make sure you're always editing.

However, this can lead to a bit of a dilemma: How do you delegate but not abdicate? Rabois said that it's a matter of measuring your own level of conviction against the consequences of that decision.

"Let people make mistakes and learn," he said. "On the other side, obviously, is where the consequences are dramatic and you have extremely high conviction that you are right, you actually can't let your junior colleague make a mistake."

The ideal way to handle that situation is just to explain your reasoning as best you can, so it doesn't seem like you're throwing your authority around just for the sake of it.

6. EDIT THE TEAM

At all costs, you should avoid the "Now that we have money, let's hire a bunch of people" inclination.

Rabois said that people often equate more people with higher horsepower. But in fact, having more people can actually get in the way of getting more work done.

When you're first starting your hiring process, Rabois said you want to look for barrels instead of ammunition. A barrel: "They can take an idea from conception ... all the way to shipping and bring people with them. That's a very cultural skill set."

Barrels require the least amount of red ink and will bring the most initiative and resourcefulness to the table, so make sure they're appreciated.

"Barrels are very difficult to find, but when you have them, give them lots of equity, promote them, take them to dinner every week, because they are virtually irreplaceable because they are also very culturally specific. A barrel at one company may not be a barrel at another company," he explained.

To decide if a person is a barrel at your company, you can expand their scope of responsibilities as far as it will go, until it breaks.

Don't worry, this isn't some crazy sort of employee hazing. Everyone has a breaking point from CEOs to interns, and the point where they break is the level they should be at or the role they should fulfill because it's the one that really pushes them.

As you gradually find out what that role is, you'll not only ensure that you're getting the full benefits out of your employees, but they'll also feel more useful.

Another little trick of the trade to finding your barrels is watching whose desk people are going to often. Chances are that person is someone in the office who is trustworthy, knowledgeable, and informative, so they could be a potential barrel.

Rabois said to promote that person and give them more responsibility.

TEAM TRANSPARENCY

With your barrels identified, aim them at your goals and have them tackle one thing at a time, rather than many.

This is a philosophy Rabois picked up from Peter Thiel (who is featured in a later chapter about competition) while working at PayPal. He explained:

> *"Most people will solve problems that they understand how to solve. Roughly speaking, they will solve B+ problems instead of A+ problems. A+ problems are high impact problems for your company, but they are difficult."*

To focus in on the A+ problems, Thiel would insist each person tackle one single thing, and they don't move on from it until it's complete. The one-thing-at-a-time approach may not work with your business, but keep in mind that the fewer tasks a person has to tackle, the more accountable they are for one thing and the more attention they have to give to it.

Another way to eliminate distractions through transparency is to create a shared, online dashboard of goals and metrics that people ideally look to on a daily basis.

"You have to create tools that enable people to make decisions at the same level you would make them yourself," said Rabois. This dashboard should be created by you, so that your team is implementing on a shared company vision.

This also means that everyone should have access to everything that's going on elsewhere in the company.

Rabois said this can be done in very literal ways like having glass walls around conference rooms and notes from all meetings available to everyone at the company. This way, no one feels like they're being left out of the loop.

MOVING YOUR COMPANY FORWARD

By gathering and simplifying information, you can better predict your output instead of your activity and adjust for improvements. But that doesn't mean you should only keep an eye out for trends and consistencies.

Rabois said it's also important to look for anomalies and what potential they may offer. He used PayPal as an example:

"One day, someone noticed that 54 of the sellers had actually handwritten into their eBay listings, 'Please pay me with PayPal,' and brought this to the attention of the executive team at the time. The first reaction from the executive team was, 'What the hell is going on? Let's get them out of the system.' Fortunately, David Sacks came back the next day and said, 'I think we found our market.'"

After encouraging the "pay with PayPal" option and including it consistently across the eBay site, PayPal was able to tap into a larger market rather than exclude one. This is just one of the many kinds of details you can't overlook.

Another one? Food.

"The best thing you can do is give people the food they want or the food that's good for them, that makes them more productive," explained Rabois.

"So it may seem like this glorious job you thought you had is more like running around being a TaskRabbit for people. But it is to take things off their plate that are a distraction so they can be high-performance machines."

THE TAKE-AWAY

Whether it's making sure you're feeding your team healthy, energizing food or teaching your receptionist the best phone etiquette, every little piece has to be in place in order for your business to run like a perfect machine, even without you at the wheel.

6

Management Advice: The Art of Balancing Competing Interests

Featuring: Ben Horowitz

When you're managing a team, your big picture view is your wheelhouse. But how do you keep cool, calm, and collected when you have to make a big decision under pressure?

As co-founder of Netscape and, more recently, Andreessen Horowitz venture capital firm, Ben Horowitz has been in these high-pressure situations many times before.

As a result, he's come up with processes and strategies to

manage a team fairly in the times when it may be the toughest.

THE BRASS "TAX" OF EMPLOYEE EQUITY

Before getting into the economics of hiring, firing, and promoting, Horowitz shared some information regarding equity in startups that may need a bit of clarification because it can get confusing if you're not familiar with the concepts.

But it's worth sticking this part out to get you set up for the rest of his presentation. In fact, this portion of Horowitz's talk at Stanford was a response to a blog post by Sam Altman. Here's the issue Altman brought up in his post:

"Most employees only have 90 days after they leave a job to exercise their options. Unfortunately, this requires money to cover the strike price and the tax bill due for the year of exercise ... This is often more cash than an employee has and so the employee often has to choose between walking away from vested options he or she can't afford to exercise or being locked into staying at the company."

This basically means that if you leave a company, for $10 million in equity, you could have to pay over $2 million to get your money. If you don't have the $2 million available now, you can't hold onto the $10 million in equity.

To Altman, this is a really archaic model and an unjust position in which to put a former employee. He offered a solution that he heard from Adam D'Angelo at Quora:

"Grant options … are exercisable for 10 years from the grant date, which should cover nearly all cases (i.e. the company will probably either go public, get acquired, or die in that time frame, and so either the employee will have the liquidity to exercise or it won't matter.)"

Altman admitted that this plan has some tricky aspects, but said that all in all it's a better solution than what's currently offered. In fact, with things being so progressive in the startup climate, why is something as important as equity still so difficult to navigate?

Horowitz said it actually used to be worse. Before 2004, the law was "If you gave somebody 10 years to exercise their options, you would never have been able to go public and you would never have been able to be acquired because you were taking an expense that was tied to your stock price."

Since 2004, though, Horowitz said, "You have to think about the people who are staying and you want to reward [them]."

If we're being honest, Horowitz said, losing all of your stock is good enough reason to stay, even if most other factors have you looking the other direction.

"That could be good news or bad news. It could be good news in that you get to keep somebody you might have lost."

HOROWITZ'S PROPOSED SOLUTION

To balance your evils, here are the two alternative options Horowitz proposed:

1. "We treat new employees with the utmost straight-forwardness and fairness and we will … give you 10 years to exercise your stock if you quit or are fired."
2. "We'll tell you up front: You are guaranteed to get your salary. For your stock to be meaningful, you must (a) vest, (b) stay until we exit or [you] have the cash to exercise, (c) make the company worth something. We do this because we massively value those who see it through and will minimize the dilutive cost of those who leave."

Horowitz said when choosing one of these two options, you have to decide how you want to run your company culture. "It's critical to think it through from everybody's perspective because when push comes to shove … that's going to change the outcome of your company."

In fact, that's the very mentality you have to keep in mind while making all big management decisions.

WHEN TO DEMOTE AND WHEN TO FIRE EXECS

When managing a startup, there are going to be problems that pop up that you might not have covered in business school or even in the early days of your startup.

One of them is having an upper-level employee who works hard, but just isn't great at his job. How do you decide whether to demote or fire him?

THE SCENARIO

An executive has worked really hard for your company, and the team likes him. All in all he is a great asset to the company culture, but he's not exemplary when it comes to the job you need him to be doing.

It's a really hard decision and to make things even more complex, Horowitz said that you have to consider the perspective of everyone involved: the CEO, the executive, and the rest of the team.

CEO's Perspective

Demotion is ideal because you can keep the employee and harness his skills in a position that's better suited for him. Also, you don't create a hole in the culture by letting him go.

Executive's Perspective

He doesn't want a demotion, but it gives an alternative to termination. Also, it's much easier to explain (and/or sugarcoat) a demotion to a future employer rather than explaining being fired.

Company Culture

If you do demote a person, how are the other people on the

team going to treat him? What shifts is this going to cause in the company's dynamics?

HOROWITZ'S SOLUTION

At the end of the day, the decision you're making doesn't just affect one person, and the results last longer than one day or one week.

"What you are really doing is saying, what does it mean to fail on the job? Particularly the highest paid, the highest compensated job in the company," Horowitz explained. "Is it good enough to put in an effort or do you have to get a result?"

After you've carefully considered the repercussions of either choice from all angles (including equity), you'll be able to balance the options.

Horowitz said to keep in mind that if you're firing someone, it's a failure: "You failed on hiring. You failed on integrating. They failed at their job ... The reason they fail on the job is you made some mistake in the hiring process and you didn't match them to the needs of your company accurately enough."

RAISING THE BAR ON RAISES

If you've ever asked for a raise, you know that it can be really intimidating and it seems like each time you do it, it's unfamiliar territory.

But as the person in charge, you have to continue to consider many factors beyond the person who's asking for a raise and ultimately create a consistent process that your employees can feel confident about.

THE SCENARIO

An excellent employee asks you for a raise.

CEO's Perspective

You want to keep this person around because she's done great work. You want to give her what she's asking for to make her happy and, of course, to gain some cool points.

Employee's Perspective

Horowitz said, "This is something they've thought about a lot. They've compared their other options. They may have an offer from another company ... It's a serious thing."

Company Culture

So, as great as the employee asking for a raise is, what about all of your other employees?

Horowitz said that if you give the person a raise who's asking for it, other people in your team may be wondering, "Okay, so I didn't ask for a raise and I didn't get a raise. They asked for a raise and they got a raise. What does that mean?"

This may lead people to believe that you aren't really

evaluating performance, but instead are just rewarding a one-time initiative.

Other employees may not be "that person" who asks for a raise, but instead are people who expect to work for companies who notice and reward their efforts as is. This will undoubtedly lead to some team turbulence.

"The cultural conclusion is that everybody in your company is going to feel that they now have a fiduciary responsibility to their family to ask for a raise all the time because if they don't, they may be missing out on a raise that they would have otherwise gotten."

This will lead to a bunch of people asking for raises all the time — something Horowitz said is called "encouraging behavior."

HOROWITZ'S SOLUTION

"You have to be formal to save your own culture," and this doesn't just apply to more established startups.

Even if you have beanbag chairs, weekly happy hours, and a Pac Man machine in the lobby, regulating the raise process and making it clear to your entire team will make you and them more accountable for performance.

Horowitz said that with his proposed process, after someone has come to you with a request for a raise, you should then evaluate her work for one quarter or six months. At the end of your evaluation, you tell her what her raise is — simple as that.

After that, there is no further discussion as you've heard her input as well as the input of the team during the evaluation. This is the best way to make the process fair and consistent.

"It means you're understanding what everyone thinks and how this is going to impact them and the culture of your company," said Horowitz.

LEARNING FROM HISTORY'S GREATEST PRACTITIONER

Horowitz said he looks to Toussaint L'Ouverture for inspiration on how to best make decisions that have an efficient, positive impact on your entire team.

L'Ouverture was a slave during one of the most brutal reigns in Haiti (then the colony of Santo Domingo). He had a vision to end slavery, take control of Haiti, and make it a first-class country.

In accomplishing the only successful slave rebellion in history, every decision he made benefited the entirety of his mission, even at times when most people would have opted for revenge against a heinous rule.

For example, after he defeated the locals, he had to decide what to do with the conquered soldiers. Rather than imprison or kill them, he considered the leaders of his opposition and the resulting culture he was working toward.

Horowitz explained, "When he conquered an army, he would take the best people from the opponent and make them generals in his army ... He wanted the expertise and to bring the culture up to a higher level."

"This is the power of looking at a situation not just from your point of view, but from the point of view of all the constituents. Even the people you hate, which is hard to do when you are a CEO and harder to do when you are leading the revolution."

Knowing that the Haitian economy depended almost solely on sugar cane, which was previously a slave economy, L'Ouverture had to then decide how to manage the acres and acres of sugar cane he'd acquired as a result of his successes.

He didn't know enough about the industry to take it in the direction he wanted it to go. So, instead of killing the slave owners, he let them keep their land and run the sugar cane plantations.

But they had to pay their workers, thereby abolishing slavery. Horowitz said that under L'Ouverture's rule, "Haiti had more export income than the U.S."

THE TAKE-AWAY

By taking inspiration from L'Ouverture and considering

all parties involved in each decision you make in the management of your company, you'll be able to keep your eye on the long view and set yourself up for future success.

Horowitz concluded, "The most important thing that you can learn, and one of the hardest things to do, is you have to discipline yourself, to see your company through the eyes of the employees, through the eyes of your partners, through the eyes of the people you are not talking to and who are not in the room."

PART III

Building Products

There comes a point where the brainstorming has to stop so the actual creation can begin.

Here are the secrets to building products — from consumer apps to hardware to enterprise software — that customers will love.

7

How to Build Products Users Love

Featuring: Kevin Hale

Do you know the secrets to building products users love? It's time to learn.

According to Kevin Hale, founder of Wufoo and partner at Y Combinator, making products users love involves focusing the bulk of your energy on the customer.

> *"My philosophy behind a lot of things that I teach in startups is, the best way to get to $1 billion is to focus on the values that help you get that first dollar to acquire that first user. If you get that right, everything else will take care of itself."*

Wufoo is an online form-builder and when you visit the site, you can already tell it's an outlier. Where most startups are constantly finding new ways to be slick and sexy, Wufoo is unabashed in its goofy persona.

As Hale said, it looks like something Fisher Price made because it's so easy to use. So easy that they have some of the world's largest companies as their clients.

Its simple, colorful appearance is not the only thing that separates Wufoo from its competitors. During fundraising, they raised about $118,000 total. But the return to their investors was about 29,561%.

To put that in perspective, the average startup raises about $25 million and the average return to investors is about 676%.

Wufoo's ROI (return on investment) is something investors dream of but rarely attain. And much of their success comes from their adamance for building relationships with their customers.

The Wufoo team constantly asks themselves: **"How do relationships work in the real world and how can we apply them to the way we run our business and build our product that way?"**

SEDUCING YOUR CUSTOMERS

It's no secret that, in human relationships, first impressions matter most. That's why when we go on a first date, we try on five outfits before we pick just the right one and maybe even study up on some talking points to sound interesting.

You need to make those initial interactions with your customers memorable – the first email, login, links, advertisements, and customer support. Hale said that all of those moments are opportunities to seduce.

For example, when you go to Wufoo's login link, there's a dinosaur on it. Hover on it, and the dinosaur will say "RARRR."

Unless you're dead inside, this simple detail will put a smile on your face. From then on, every time you login, you'll associate positive emotions with their product.

Seducing your customers doesn't have to involve some glossy campaign. As long as you think about what emotions you elicit on your user's face, you're heading in the right direction.

TREAT CUSTOMER SUPPORT LIKE A MARRIAGE

Hale took many customer service lessons from marriage psychologist John Gottman. Gottman is famous for being able to predict (with freakish accuracy) whether a couple is going to divorce. He just needs to watch them fight for 15 minutes.

ANTICIPATING CUSTOMERS' NEEDS

According to Gottman, in human relationships everybody

fights about the exact same things: money, kids, sex, time, etc. The same goes for customer support complaints.

- Money = this costs too much or I'm having trouble with credit cards
- Kids = user's client
- Sex = performance (how long you're up and how fast)
- Etc. = competition and partnerships

Knowing these customer service triggers helps you anticipate what complaints your users will bring to you, which in turn will make you better equipped to solve their problems.

ALWAYS RESPOND TO YOUR CUSTOMERS

Gottman also said that couples often break up because of four major causes: criticism, contempt, defensiveness, and stonewalling. Stonewalling is one of the worst things a person can do in a relationship, yet startups do it often.

Stonewalling is when you have a lot of customer support calls coming in and you refuse to respond. Not meeting your customers' needs is the "biggest cause of churn in the early stages of startups," said Hale.

EVERYONE ON YOUR TEAM SHOULD DO CUSTOMER SUPPORT

Another practice that separates Wufoo from a typical startup was the integration of customer support into the role of software development. They uphold values they feel aren't discussed enough, like responsibility, accountability, humility, and modesty. They call it SDD (Support Driven Development).

Jared Spool, a user interface engineer, largely informed these values. He said that there's a direct correlation between how much time software developers spend directly exposed to users and the quality of their designs.

So Wufoo spent 30% of their engineering time on internal tools to help with customer support.

As a result, Hale said, their developers were "getting exposed to our users [for] four to eight hours every single week," changing the way they built software.

"We redesigned our documentation over and over again, A/B tested it constantly. One iteration of our documentation page reduced customer support by 30% overnight," Hale said.

By concentrating on customer service, the product team actually had a 30% reduction of their workload.

EMOTIONS ARE IMPORTANT

Wufoo prioritizes customer support because it's integral to every step of the conversion process. If you fail at customer service, conversions just don't happen. That's why frequent customer service experimentation is a staple activity for the Wufoo team.

THE LITTLE EXPERIMENT THAT COULD

Not being face-to-face with the bulk of their users created an emotional disconnect that hindered the customer support process.

The Wufoo team addressed this by adding a drop-down to their support form that asked users about their current emotional state. Think of it as the predecessor to Facebook's emoticon statuses.

The team expected this experiment to fail. But not only was the support field filled out 75.8% of the time, users also filled out the emotional state drop-down 78.1% of the time. How the users felt about a problem was just as important as the technical solutions the Wufoo team provided.

THE SECRET TO GETTING NICER USERS

Working in customer support is extremely stressful. You're basically getting paid to have people yell at you for eight hours every day. Customer support workers often have the least amount of power to affect change in an organization, but they receive the majority of the users' frustrations.

Because Wufoo had their software team doing support work, users became less frustrated. This was because they were interacting with people who could actually do something about their problems. But, providing an emotional outlet brought it to another level.

People started being nicer to the support team as a result. Users became more rational and in turn made the Wufoo team's job more pleasant.

THE TAKE-AWAY

Your customer interactions, whether through UI or customer service, are all part of a larger relationship you're forming with them.

Take care to make their entire experience pleasant, and in return, they'll see your company and product as something well worth their time and money.

8

Competition Is for Losers

Featuring: Peter Thiel

What does competition actually look like in the startup world? How can young businesses be competitive? And is our society's relationship with competition healthy?

Peter Thiel — co-founder of PayPal, early investor in Facebook, and co-founder of Founders Fund — answered these questions and more during his Stanford University lecture.

CREATING VALUE

Comparing the size of the airline industry to the size of the search industry, you would come to the conclusion that airlines are more important than search. But Thiel points out that the airline industry's profit margins are significantly less than those of the search industry.

In the airline industry, the companies make money, go bankrupt, get recapitalized, and then that cycle repeats itself. This is reflected in the combined market capitalization of the airline industry, which is close to just a quarter of Google's. So even though the search industry is much smaller than air travel, it's actually more valuable.

So how do you go about creating value when you first start a business, and what makes a company valuable? Thiel said you have to create something of value and capture some fraction of the value you've created.

MONOPOLIES VS PERFECT COMPETITION

Thiel sees the business world as a binary. On one end of the spectrum, you have industries that are perfectly competitive, and at the other end of the spectrum are monopolies. Thiel said, "There is shockingly little that is in between."

MONOPOLIES

Monopolies are more stable, long-term businesses, and they have more capital. And if you get a creative monopoly for inventing something new, it often means you've created something really valuable.

The other side of things is perfect competition.

76

PERFECT COMPETITION

According to Investopedia, perfect competition is "a market structure in which the following five criteria are met:

1. All firms sell an identical product.
2. All firms are price takers — they cannot control the market price of their product.
3. All firms have a relatively small market share.
4. Buyers have complete information about the product being sold and the prices charged by each firm.
5. The industry is characterized by freedom of entry and exit."

Pro

Perfect competition is always easy to model and it's efficient, especially in a world where things are static.

Con

Perfect competition doesn't make money when a lot of competition is involved.

THE LIES WE TELL

MONOPOLIES PRETEND TO HAVE LOTS OF COMPETITION

According to Thiel, monopolies tend to lie. They don't want the government to regulate them, so they won't call themselves a monopoly. What do they do to escape scrutiny? They pretend to have a lot of competition.

For example, Google has a 66% market share of the search industry. But you'll never hear them describe themselves as a search engine anymore. Sometimes they call themselves an advertising company and sometimes they refer to themselves as a technology company.

There's a good reason for this renaming. The technology market is valued at close to $1 trillion. So Google's narrative is that they're competing with all the car companies with their self-driving cars, they're competing with Apple on TVs and smartphones, they're competing with Microsoft on office products, and they're competing with Amazon on cloud services.

They've positioned themselves in the expansive technology market where there's competition everywhere. That's how they escape the threat of regulating their monopoly.

NON-MONOPOLIES PRETEND TO HAVE NO COMPETITION

The companies on the other end of the spectrum, which exist in a highly competitive industry, are also tempted to lie because they may not make any money otherwise.

They'll say they're doing something unique that is less competitive than it looks. They want to separate themselves from the rest of the herd and attract capital. Thiel said that they do this to increase their perceived value.

For example, a new restaurant that no one wants to invest in (because restaurants are notoriously bad investments) will be tempted to rebrand themselves. They'll claim that they're the only British food restaurant in Palo Alto. That's too small of a market. But because of the way they talk about their place in the market, it seems like they have a monopoly on British food in Palo Alto.

THE RESULT?

"In a world where monopolists pretend not to have monopolies and non-monopolies pretend to have monopolies, it seems like the difference between the two is very small. But in reality, the real difference is vast. These lies produce a distortion of the business world."

Look at the big tech companies: Apple, Google, Microsoft, and Amazon. They have built up cash for years, producing incredibly high profit margins.

Thiel said that the U.S. tech industry has been so financially successful because it's prone to creating monopoly-like businesses. These companies accumulate so much cash that they don't even know what to do with it beyond a certain point.

GO AFTER SMALL MARKETS

If you're a startup, you want to have a monopoly because monopolies possess a large share of the market. But how do you get there?

Thiel advised beginning with a really small market, taking

over said market, and then expanding that market in concentric circles.

The biggest mistake you can make as a young startup is going after a giant market from the get-go. That signifies that you haven't defined categories correctly. And you're going to be dealing with too much competition in one way or another.

Even Amazon started with just a bookstore. Their selling point was that they had all the books in the world for sale online. After they established themselves as a bookstore, they expanded into different types of e-commerce.

In the tech world, there's this feeling that, in technology's history, every moment happens only once, so your company needs to be unique.

In Thiel's words: "You don't want to be the fourth online pet food company. You don't want to be the tenth solar panel company … All unhappy companies are alike because they failed to escape the essential sameness in competition."

"The next Mark Zuckerberg won't build a social network and the next Larry Page won't be building a search engine, and the next Bill Gates won't be building an operating system. If you are copying these people, you are not learning from them," Thiel said.

LAST MOVER ADVANTAGE

You want technology with a magnitude that is 10x better than the next best thing, and you want it to last.

He disagreed with the notion espoused by Silicon Valley that you need to be the first mover to be successful in business. Instead, you need to be the best.

Thiel pointed out some tech companies whose iconic fame comes from being last instead of being first: "Microsoft was the last operating system, at least for many decades. Google was the last search engine. Facebook will be valuable if it turns out to be the last of social networking sites."

The reason these last movers succeed is because "most of the value in these companies exists far in the future."

Thiel added, "If you do a discounted cash flow analysis of the business, you'll look at all these profit streams. You have a growth rate. The growth rate's much higher that the discount rate, and so most of the value exists far in the future."

When Thiel was at PayPal in 2001, their growth rate was about 100% per year. And they had been in business for a little over two years. They were discounting future cash flows by 30%, but in actuality, about three quarters of the value of the business as of 2001 came from cash flows in the years 2011 and beyond.

According to Thiel, you get similar results if you analyze

Silicon Valley tech companies like Airbnb, Twitter, Facebook, and any emerging Internet companies. The math will tell you that 85% of the value is coming from cash flows in years 2024 and beyond. So, he said, we need to stop overvaluing growth and undervaluing durability.

Everybody wants to have a huge breakthrough in technology — a eureka moment. But unless your breakthrough is the final breakthrough, you won't last.

Thiel explained that your only other option is to make a breakthrough and constantly improve on it at a pace that no one can keep up with. You need to think about who will be the leading company 10 to 20 years from now.

COMPETITION IS FOR "LOSERS"

Not every successful invention or innovation makes the inventor rich. In fact, scientists are seldom adequately rewarded for their advances to how we live. Thiel noted that the smartest physicist of the 20th century, Albert Einstein, wasn't a billionaire.

For science, the rationale is that scientists aren't interested in making money; instead they're supposed to be doing the work for charitable reasons.

Thiel did not say that people should always be motivated by money but thinks we should be more critical of these rationalizations. He questions the obscure explanations for why certain innovations get rewarded and others don't.

Software is seen as the most valuable thing in the world because so many people have made buckets of money in the industry. The logic is that, if people at Twitter make billions of dollars, then Twitter must be worth more than anything Einstein did. This type of rationalization is dangerous, according to Thiel.

"We think of losers as the people who are slow on the track team in high school or do a little less well on standardized tests and don't get into the right schools," Thiel said. Losers are seen as people who can't compete.

Thiel wants us to rethink and revalue this concept and consider the possibility that the competition itself is off. It's no longer a form of validation.

"I think it's more than just an intellectual blind spot, but also a psychological blind spot, where we find ourselves very attracted to competition, and in one form or another we find it reassuring if other people do things. And this is a very problematic thing that we need to always think through and try to overcome," Thiel said.

When Thiel was in eighth grade, one of his friends wrote "I know you're going to get into Stanford" in his yearbook.

He did, in fact, attend Stanford Law School years later. Then he ended up at a big New York law firm where, as he put it, "from the outside everybody wanted to get in and on the inside everybody wanted to leave."

He didn't like the dynamic and left the firm after seven months. He said that it's important to pause in the midst of things and ask yourself if the tournament continues to make sense as you keep going.

His colleagues applauded him for leaving, even though for him it was a simple choice. "So much of people's identities got wrapped up in winning these competitions that they somehow lost sight of what was important, what was valuable," he said.

THE TAKE-AWAY

Competition does make you better at whatever it is you're doing — that's true. But Thiel is concerned about what often comes with it. He said, "You stop asking some bigger questions about what's truly important and truly valuable."

As Thiel concluded, "Don't always go through the tiny little door that everyone's trying to rush through, maybe go around the corner and go through the vast gate that nobody is taking."

9

Designing Hardware for the Internet of Things

Featuring: Hosain Rahman

According to Jawbone founder and CEO Hosain Rahman, the Internet of Things has gotten cluttered. Here's how his company is looking to change that.

As Rahman explained in his recent Stanford lecture, the process at Jawbone stays really big picture until it starts to get to the end, and that's part of what gives the hardware company an edge.

From their UP 24 fitness tracker to the Jambox Bluetooth speaker, Jawbone has continued to make gadgets and wearables that are at the top of their game, aspiring to design hardware products that people can't live without.

With each of their products, Rahman said, "I always like to start with the broadest thinking ... We think that the conversation has shifted even beyond design into beauty. It's the intersection of engineering meets beauty. The whole point is to help people have a better life with technology."

LOOKING FORWARD

Rahman said that most of the chaos surrounding the Internet of Things has to do with the fact that all of these apps and gadgets that we're plugged into aren't talking to each other, so they're confined to their own feature set.

"It's really confusing for the user," he said. "We think that there is a desperate need for an organizing principle around all of this. This is the core of when we start to think about how we build and [find] opportunities to create products."

The team continues to look forward to ensure that they're not just creating hardware of the moment, but of the generation. Rahman said, "What happens when we can dream in future? We really try to live into tomorrow ... [and] the thing that we build today is a gradual stepping stone to graduate users."

JAWBONE'S TWO MAIN PRINCIPLES

1. IT'S NOT ABOUT THE THINGS. IT'S ABOUT THE USERS.

"What we believe is that when you have things that are on your body 24/7, they become a perfect context engine for everything in the world around you."

2. YOU HAVE TO BE GOOD AT THE FULL STACK.

Rahman said the "full stack" is the combination of software, services, and data. When these three are exceptional, he said, you can unlock the potential of something that works with the individual user and the rest of the world.

EVERYTHING IS A SYSTEM

For Jawbone, their process of creating new hardware is to keep things super creative and open for as long as they can. Step by step, they narrow in on their vision, all along keeping in mind that what they're creating is going to become part of a larger system.

EXPLORATION

This is the brainstorming phase where the team dreams big and imagines products to fit into the direction that they see the world going. They think on what the brand stands for and how they can disrupt the market.

EARLY VALIDATION

The concepts that they've dreamed up really start to hit paper.

At this point, they're predicting where the product can fit into the market and they're attempting to prove their theories.

CONCEPT

They continue to get closer and closer to fruition by mapping out the experience and how they're going to tell the story. They're really starting to explore what's possible.

PLANNING

They start asking themselves, "What are some of the tradeoffs we're going to have to make? What are the constraints?" This will help them further focus the product.

DEVELOPMENT

During this phase, they merge their teams and talents and start to learn from their users.

Rahman said they have to ask, "What have we achieved? What haven't we achieved? What have we learned from our users? How does that change what we're thinking?"

CONTINUED INNOVATION

They launch the product and continue learning from users. They see what users think and where their thoughts stand in comparison to the direction they predicted.

To really explore their products further, Jawbone uses what they call "Demo Friday." They treat it like first-round funding and get people to pitch their ideas to the outside world.

IT'S ALL ABOUT THE WHYS

To stay grounded in your company's mission statement and ensure that your end product is solving the problem that you set out to solve, Rahman said you have to keep asking yourself:

- **Why are we doing this?**
- **Why does this exist?**
- **What problem does it solve?**

From research and development to industrial design, each team has to take these questions into consideration as they pertain to their expertise.

During the concept phase at Jawbone, Rahman said that they take the project to their Product Experience team, which would be a conventional design team anywhere else. They're not building the hardware, but their job is hugely important.

Rahman said, "We have writers on that team. Storytellers. We have ID people who are genius creators. We have amazing app level designers, graphic designers, everything. It's all one team and we call that Product Experience. Their job is to unify us as one organization."

RESOLVING THE WHYS

When your project is truly successful, you've resolved all of the questions and problems you've been iterating on since the beginning of your process. Rahman calls it all the Hero Experience. When you've resolved those questions, then you can start to examine your competition and find product-market fit.

This is where those tradeoffs you were considering before really start to come into action. Do you sacrifice product size for battery life? Do you use that material if the color you want isn't available? In other words, it's time to dig into the nitty gritty and make the final decisions.

But Rahman said you still have to keep in mind, "Does it actually cross enough things off our list? Does it meet that minimum viability?" And in the bigger picture, he always wants to ensure that they're not creating a one-off product.

"We have to see a broader vision. This is part of the creation experience. We look at where we think the world is moving and think about how this [product] is going to be a stepping stone to that ultimate end vision."

TALKING TO USERS

As recently as five years ago, Rahman said that no one wanted a Bluetooth speaker for $199; there simply wasn't a market for it. But they waited and questioned users.

He explained that it's important not to ask them leading questions because, at the end of the day, people will tell you what you want to hear.

"No one's going to tell you what to build. If they do, then they should do it and not you. You're the one who's making that decision. You've got the thesis. You've got the creative idea. You've got the innovation. You've got to use these people to help you make it better and to refine your thinking."

To refine your thinking, you've got to storyboard. Rather than just talking about the user story, draw it out. It doesn't have to be in extreme detail, but just enough to see movement for movement what their process looks like so you can ensure that your product isn't being forced in a direction where it's not welcome.

He said that creating a storyboard also helps to map out constraints: "My experience has been [that] constraints are really great because they serve as opportunities to resolve, to refine, to simplify, and push you to find the right answer that will solve the user problem in the simplest way."

THE SYSTEM IS A FLAGSHIP

The end goal for all of Jawbone's products is to fit within their system and the direction that the world is going.

Rahman said that they ask themselves, "'What is the user problem that we solve through this experiment?' Whether it's in hardware, software, data, platform, whatever it is, once we solve it, people can't live without it."

To create this hardware that people can't live without, their system is key. When they work within their system, "[the hardware gets] to a level of emotional connection where you feel that without it you're lost ... Those are the principles that govern all these things. We have to keep asking ourselves those questions. Is it doing that?"

THE TAKE-AWAY

Rahman said that, rather than thinking of themselves as a hardware or software company, they think of themselves as an experiences company. "It's not just about this physical device or that feature. It's about the system. It's about how the pieces come together."

With the system perfected, they can start to streamline the chaos in the Internet of Things and really create an intuitive, fluid experience.

10

Why You Should Build for the Enterprise

Featuring: Aaron Levie

Do a search of "Enterprise vs. Consumer Startups" and you'll get endless, contradictory opinions of what each of these terms mean and which is better. But now just might be the perfect time to start an enterprise software company.

Aaron Levie began his lecture on building for the enterprise by making his way to the front of the classroom at Stanford to the tune of "Eye of the Tiger."

That's just the kind of pump up an enterprise lecture needs in a room full of students looking for the fame and fortune of Mark Zuckerberg.

Levie said when he and co-founder Dylan Smith were starting their cloud-based storage company Box a decade ago before even finishing school, they had to make a big decision: would it be a consumer or enterprise startup?

CONSUMER VS ENTERPRISE

The idea for Box arose from the simple need to share files in the early days of the Internet becoming a more common tool.

As young 20-something college dropouts with a really early version of their product, Levie and Smith viewed their options like this:

"When you do a consumer startup, it's basically lots of fun. You have parties all the time, it's just super exciting. Then in the enterprise, you are battling these large incumbents; it's a fairly thankless model because people just generally hate enterprise software."

Thus is the hard sell for enterprise software. But money talks, and compared to the $35 billion spent on mobile apps each year (either through paid apps or advertising), there is $3.7 trillion spent on enterprise IT.

Levie and Smith had the realization that "[w]e are going to be fighting to get consumers to pay a few dollars a month. And Google, Microsoft, and Apple will try to make this product free over time … But in enterprise, it's not about them trying to save money on IT. [Companies] are either trying to increase productivity or they are trying to increase business. So the value equation is very different."

Enterprise startups will generally see a more incremental, stable growth rather than a viral boom. It's a process that builds at a steady pace and demands satisfaction from users and organizations every step of the way. Entire companies build upon the structure of enterprise software and organize their workflows around it.

By taking the enterprise route and getting bigger and bigger clients over the past decade, Box has managed to build an adaptable business model for the enterprise.

Today, Box hosts 27 million users at 240,000 businesses small and large. Like, really large: Toyota, GE, Food Network, etc.

Their success and the success of future enterprise software companies is owed, at least in part, to some key shifts in the technology landscape.

THE TIMES THEY ARE A-CHANGIN'

Changes in technology have endless ripple effects that impact every tech company out there, and enterprise software is no exception.

APPS MOVING TO THE CLOUD

Before the cloud became commonly used, business software

was a redundant, tedious task being implemented again and again in different places. And the transition to the cloud in the enterprise world was not as swift as in the consumer startup world.

Enterprises work with a variety of other big businesses and, with so many moving parts, a jump to new technology is a big one. It has to be carefully planned and executed, so Levie and Smith had to make their product worth the leap.

To do that, they played by a "different set of rules" with the help of outspoken investor (also early in his career) Mark Cuban. The Box founders "looked at all of the factors that are true with the enterprise" and decided they were going to do the opposite.

Levie said, "We are going to find what has changed in the technology world ... and build a newer and better software company. That was the decision we embarked on, the path we embarked on eight years ago. And that is why we have been focused on enterprise."

CHEAPER ON-DEMAND COMPUTING

Again, money talks. From a time of all things tech-related carrying the stigma of an extra expense, cheaper computing made what was once extraneous, mandatory.

It became easier to adopt new technology, even for large companies, which means that smaller software companies were finally able to go after those larger markets.

With the price barrier being broken down in the world of on-demand computing, there also needed to be another layer of accessibility for users.

Rather than fully customized platforms, the trend was moving to standardized software — think of the difference from your MySpace page to your Facebook profile.

People no longer wanted completely open platforms, but instead a consistent software with a layer of customization built on top.

MOBILE DEVICES

With people operating so much of their online lives from the palm of their hands, software is now user-led. There are more people with smartphones, leading to more people online, which makes changes in technology even more drastic. Enterprises had to react to these disruptions.

Levie offered this example:

"In the healthcare space, every single healthcare institution is trying to find ways of building more personalized experiences, more predictive experiences. They want to have medicine be adapted to the individual. How are our healthcare providers going to get connected to one another so doctors can make better decisions? All of these things are going to require new enterprise software to power these businesses and industries."

"Every industry is going to have a technology component of what they do. Enterprises are not going to be able to survive in the future if they do not get good at technology."

BUILDING AN ADAPTABLE ENTERPRISE

How does your enterprise adapt to these changes?

Here's an even better question: How do you start an enterprise that is adaptable?

START SMALL

By finding tiny gaps in existing products, you can make that small space your niche, learn it inside and out, and completely own that wedge of the market.

"What you want to start to do is say, 'We will take this sliver of a problem and we are going to make the user experience on that incredible,'" said Levie.

This way, when you're starting out, you're not even worrying about the big guys until you completely own your space enough to grow and branch out.

SPOT TECHNOLOGY DISRUPTIONS

"You have to look for new enabling technologies or major trends ... that create a wide gap between how things are done and how they can be done," advised Levie.

This is not only key to finding that little sliver for your business to fit in, it's also important for realizing new opportunities for your business before the competition catches on. In the tech world, major progress affects all of the players.

FIND ASYMMETRIES

There are lots of perks to being the little guy — find them and use them.

"You want to do things that incumbents can't or won't do because either the economics don't make sense for them, the economics are so unusual, or because technically they can't," explained Levie.

Before you do this, though, do your research and find exactly where your incumbents can't afford to drop their prices or personalize their UX, then fill in those gaps.

FIND OUTLIERS

Examining those users around the cusp of your industry can give you just the edge you need to take your next steps. Levie said, "Find the unique characteristics of those customers."

"If you find customers that are working in the future, you will be able to work with them to find what is missing in the future." Then ask yourself, "How do we build technology that supports all these new use cases that are going to emerge?"

If you work with those outliers as early adopters, you can study them to see how your product can evolve.

This will also help you to distill your overall customer needs and narrow in on the best solution. As Levie explained, this may be one that they need, not necessarily one that they want.

THE TAKE-AWAY

With your user at the center of your product's DNA and an eye on the long game, enterprise software is a great place to be right now.

With the rapid pace at which new technology is being produced, there are even more gaps to fill with potential lasting solutions for each of them.

PART IV

Reaching Your Audience

Once you've built your product, you've got to get it out into the market. Here's how to harness feedback from early users and attention from the media to land your first big customers.

flyers?

11

How to Run a Successful User Interview

Featuring: Emmett Shear

If you're going to impress your users, you have to know what they're thinking. It turns out the best way to find that out is just to ask.

Emmett Shear admits that, in their first business venture together, he and co-founder Justin Kan created a product without a solid use case.

But later they wised up and founded Justin.tv, which later became Twitch — "the world's leading video platform and community for gamers."

If you're unfamiliar with this new form of live feed gaming entertainment, it's basically where, instead of playing a video game or watching your friends play on your couch, you watch someone else from your computer or broadcast your own game play.

The platform didn't start out as this, however. Justin.tv (Twitch's first form) was a site where you could broadcast your life. Shear explained, "If you wanted to run a live 24/7 reality television show about your life, we had the website for you."

But they needed to get bigger and reach a broader audience and to do that, they needed use cases to find where these people were. In the end, in order to grow, they had to pivot.

"There were two directions that seemed promising," said Shear. "One was mobile and one was gaming."

TALK TO THE RIGHT USERS

Shear was in charge of getting the scoop on the gaming side of things, which of course was the direction the company wound up going. That was the first time they started to talk to users.

Shear said that this was especially crucial for them to do early on because, "While I loved watching gaming videos, I was very aware that neither I nor anyone else in the company knew anything about broadcasting video games."

To figure out how to acquire content and start broadcasting, they had to reach out to the people who'd actually be using the site.

As their idea became more tangible, "We determined that the broadcasters were the most important people because, when we went and looked into the market, we looked into what determined why people watched a certain stream or went to a certain website. They would just follow the content," Shear said.

So they had to investigate the people who were putting the content out there.

Figuring out which group in their audience was most influential to their business was important. But to get the entire scope of things, they had to identify and interview other groups, as well.

"It comes down to thinking really hard and using your judgment to figure out who you are really building this for," said Shear.

He added that picking a user comes above all else. "Before you think about who you should ask, or what the features should be, just think about who is going to use this app? ... Who am I going to talk to? ... And where am I going to find them?"

Interviews will give you these insights, where stats and data just can't.

INTERVIEWING – ROUND 1

When interviewing people about your product, it should be all about them — not your app.

Don't ask them anything regarding features you're thinking about or even other competing products in the space.

Shear said that those kinds of questions will distract you from solving the problem because you're getting answers based on the assumption that people know what they want, but that's not the case.

People know the problem they have, and sure they'll tell you how they think it should be fixed for themselves, but it's your job to create a product that solves the problems of your entire audience.

"You [can] get the horseless carriage effect where you're asked for a faster horse instead of being asked to design the actual solution to the problem."

Shear added, "So you want to stay as far away from features [in the first interview] as possible because the things they tell you feel overwhelmingly real. When you have a real user asking you for a feature, it's very hard to say no to them because here's a real person who really has this problem."

After you've talked to a wide spectrum of 6–8 potential users, Shear said it's best to move on to the next phase, as anything after that is likely to be a lot of repeat information.

NARROW IN ON YOUR IDEAS

You're no longer completely shooting in the dark at this point. Now you can literally put faces to your potential users and start figuring out the exact problems that your product is going to solve. You can also start brainstorming how that's going to happen.

Shear said that a great place to start, if possible, is to build on top of existing platforms. So, if you want to build a new email experience, maybe start with a Gmail extension to test your idea before trying to build an entirely new platform.

When narrowing your idea, you're not just trying to create something that people will like, and certainly not just something that people will tell you they like.

Instead, you want it to be something that they would buy (download, view, etc) and even better, something so good that they stop using another product in that space and replace it with yours.

To test your theory, you can build a quick mockup of your product for people to test. But even if you don't have the capacity to do a mockup or prototype, Shear said you should go into your second round of interviews with your more focused goal in mind.

INTERVIEWING – ROUND 2

In lieu of showing your interviewees an actual version of your product, which Shear advises against, he said in round two you can opt to draw out diagrams of what it might look like so that people can understand the workflow.

> *"You want to learn what's already in their heads. You want to avoid putting things there."*

You could think of it as leading questions in journalism. When you're interviewing people, you need their honest opinions — not what you want to hear. Because even if you lead them to say, "Yeah this is the best app ever. I'd totally use it," that doesn't mean they actually will when the time comes.

When interviewing, you're always searching for problems from your interviewee, not validation and definitely not a solution.

Putting them in the position of just commenting on whether they like the app is giving them an easy out and not providing you with any useful information.

If your product is something that you intend to charge people for, that's a bigger challenge with a bigger payoff because you can try and get them to pay you just from seeing the mockups or the test site.

Shear said, at this stage especially, "Get people to give you their credit card and I guarantee you they are actually interested in the feature."

DISSECTING THE FEEDBACK

After your interviews, you're going to have gathered a ton of information. Rather than tackle it comment by comment or just focus on one feature someone mentioned, you've got to get the big picture.

This should include your users, but also your competitors' users, and even non-users who aren't in your space at all.

YOUR USERS

With Twitch, Shear said they looked at all of their user feedback and found trends and commonalities. For their business, they were able to narrow down the essence of the major concerns into five statements that were easier to diagnose.

Most of the issues from their own users were a matter of interface or function. "When you talk to detailed users of your product, they come back to you with very detailed things about features because they get mired in the features," said Shear. "You have to sort of read between the lines."

COMPETITORS' USERS

Shear said the information they learned from their own users was of course interesting, but not as helpful as it could have been.

"If you thought that [we set out to] address these problems, you would be wrong. People who are using your service already are willing to put up with all these issues, which kind of means that these are probably not the biggest problems."

No matter how big any of these users' issues were, they weren't big enough to deter them from the site. So in the grand picture of Twitch, they were rather small issues.

In order to broaden your scope, you have to look at people who are using competing services or those who have left yours. These are the people who will point out the really raw pain points that your current audience doesn't care about or overlooks.

When they talked to competitor's users, they got totally different feedback than what they got from their own and it was about more general issues, rather than interface and functional problems.

Shear said, "We focused on this stuff because this was the stuff that was so bad that people weren't even willing to use our service."

NON-USERS

This is the powerhouse for ultimate expansion. These are people who are not thinking about your brand at all, so they take the most convincing and require the most questioning.

Shear said, "In the case of gaming broadcasting, almost

everyone is a non-user. The majority of people you are competing with are non-users," so they were particularly important for Twitch's growth.

"If all you do is look at your competitors and talk to people who use your competitors' products, you can never expand. You're not learning things that help you expand the size of the market. You want to talk to people who aren't even trying to use these things yet."

Again, when you're talking to these people, you're not trying to discover the features they'd add or even how they would use your product.

You're trying to learn about their lives to find issues that they're having and the goals they're trying to accomplish. Then you find out where your product can fit into that.

INTERVIEW TIPS

DO IT IN PERSON

Shear said, "Email interviews are basically useless." When you're interacting with someone in person or via Skype, people may ramble into places that are really insightful, which you can then explore further.

RECORD THEM

When you record your interview, you don't have to take notes, which can be disruptive. Also, you can play that recording for your team later, so you can pitch your new ideas with the support of the user feedback in video (or at least audio).

Talking to users should be one of the first steps in creating your startup and will continue to guide you in each decision you make for your company.

Unless the product you're creating is just for yourself, the people who you're creating for should have the first say. And if you've solved their problems in the right way, you can have the last.

THE TAKE-AWAY

User feedback is valuable, but insight from non-users is even more so.

To really understand your market and find opportunities for growth, interview people beyond your user list and follow the tips above to make the most of your time with them.

12

Getting Press the Right Way

Featuring: Justin Kan

Attracting media attention can be tricky. Here's some advice that will increase your likelihood of success.

From Kiko and Justin.tv to Twitch, Justin Kan's ventures have received press coverage on tech sites and beyond, and his advice has definitely been learned first-hand through trial and error.

From his own experience, he knows that, before you start reaching out to news sources at all, you have to ask yourself some basic questions. Once you have answers for these questions, you'll be better able to respond to queries from the press when they come a knockin'.

Here are the questions you should ask yourself:

WHAT IS YOUR GOAL?

What do you want people to come away from the story knowing about your startup?

Make sure you keep these business goals in mind before talking about your company so you can speak about it clearly and concisely. "Um"s and "you know"s don't read well in an interview.

WHO DO YOU WANT TO REACH?

Consider your audience before reaching out to news outlets. Writers want material that will interest their readers, so make sure that you're pitching in places where your story is likely to have an audience.

Kan gave an example of how he went about finding an audience for Twitch PR:

"Twitch TV … is like ESPN for gamers, kind of like a live stream community for gamers. Our goal was to reach the gaming industry … whether they were developers or advertisers. [We wanted them] to think about us as an important place where influencers were, so we really targeted industry trades and game dev blogs — stuff that the industry was reading."

Kan suggests that it's best to handle PR yourself rather than hiring an agency, at least early on. "It's generally not a good use of money, especially in the early days [to hire a firm]."

He said that most firms can only help you with contacts and logistics. They can't create your story.

WHAT TYPE OF STORY ARE YOU PITCHING?

After you have an idea for your story and the audience(s) you want to tap into, it's time to figure out what type of story you're bringing to the table.

Once you know which of these you fulfill, you'll be better able to pitch your story in a convincing way.

Product Launches: The beginning is always a good place to start.

Fundraising: People love a good financial success story.

Milestones/Metrics: Did you make a lot of revenue in one week? Numbers talk, so that could be news.

Business Overviews: Startup stories are always great reads. But more often than not, this coverage only comes when you're a bit beyond the early stages.

Stunts: Think guerrilla advertising.

Hiring Announcements: Like when former Etsy designer

Cap Watkins became BuzzFeed's first VP of Design, that's big news.

Guest Posts: Contribute your own voice to the outlets your audiences are reading by writing a guest post.

STEP-BY-STEP PITCH PROCESS

Even after you've nailed down your goals, found an audience, and picked which type of story you want to present, you're still going to have to actually pitch your story to someone who will hopefully write about it.

Kan shared some step-by-step advice on how to do that:

1. THINK OF A STORY

Before you pitch your story, Kan said, "What you really need to think about objectively is, 'If I wasn't the founder of this company, would I want to read a story about what I'm pitching?'"

2. GET INTRODUCED

It's best to get introduced to a reporter through someone else. Think about someone who has already covered a friend or fellow entrepreneur who you know and ask your contact to make the introduction.

3. SET A DATE

Give the reporter at least four to seven days to write and publish your story — more if you can.

4. REACH OUT

A lot can get lost in translation over email. Get a commitment from the reporter to meet face-to face or at least talk on the phone, if you can.

5. PITCH THEM

When pitching your story, write out bullet points of what you want covered. This is what Olivia Pope calls "controlling the narrative." Yes, that was a reference to the T.V. show *Scandal*.

6. FOLLOW UP

Leave things on a good note before the launch and thank the reporter for his/her time. Also, tie up any possible loose ends by confirming potential lingering details: names of founders, date of launch, etc.

7. LAUNCH YOUR NEWS

The final step is to share your big announcement. And ideally the reporters are publishing the articles you pitched at the same time.

DON'T CONFUSE PRESS WITH SUCCESS

In your pursuit of press, Kan said it's important to keep in mind that a lot of media coverage does not a good product make:

> "Getting press is like a vanity metric. It feels like you're being successful because many successful companies like Facebook are covered in the press all the time, but it doesn't actually mean you're

successful. It doesn't actually mean you're making money, getting users, or making those users happy."

THE TAKE-AWAY

Media attention in and of itself does not mean your startup is successful.

Still, if you're keeping your users happy, making a stellar product, and maintaining good relationships with reporters, you're definitely on the right track to getting the kind of coverage you're looking for.

13

How to Land Early Customers

Featuring: Tyler Bosmeny

When you're selling to customers, knowing how to talk about your business concisely (as well as when to stop talking and just listen) is key.

Tyler Bosmeny, co-founder and CEO of education startup Clever, has discovered in his life of sales that it's important to search out the innovators.

Sure, this is the smallest market — just 2.5% of the total population — but it's the most pivotal and most likely to take your calls as an early company.

FINDING YOUR SALES LEADS

If you start there, he said you'll start to realize that this is a numbers game.

At Clever, Bosmeny's initial contact list was 400 companies made up of personal connections, friends of friends, and cold emails. But of course, the people you know personally are always going to be your strongest supporters.

It can be hard to meet new people when you're heads down building a company, but Bosmeny said one of the best ways to meet potential customers and partners is at conferences — and not the big ones.

The smaller, less glamorous conferences can give you more opportunities to make lasting, one-on-one connections with people.

MAKING THE SALE

BE SURE TO LISTEN

As you're going through your call list of 400 people, Bosmeny said the most important thing to remember during your conversations is to shut up.

> *"The best salespeople in the world ... don't talk a lot. They ask a lot of questions to then fully understand the person's problem."*

DON'T FORGET TO FOLLOW UP

After that initial conversation, it's all about the follow up. Persistent follow up.

During his talk at Stanford, Bosmeny showed a timeline of what his follow up can look like on a good day, and it's clear that a lot of emails and calls go unanswered.

You'll run into people who are difficult to keep tabs on, but that doesn't always mean the answer is no.

AVOID THE MAYBES AND IFS

What you do want to avoid is being dragged along on a "maybe."

"Your goal should be to get people to a 'yes' or 'no' as quickly as you can," he explained. Maybes can be a huge time suck.

Another word that may cause you some grief is "if." Some people will only want to use your product if you add a new feature.

Bosmeny has two solutions for these predicaments that will help you to avoid creating a one-off feature (which is never a good idea):

1. Sign a sales agreement, which includes that you'll add that feature after the prospect becomes a paying customer.
2. Better yet, say that you'll wait to get validation from other customers that this is a need for them as well.

STEER CLEAR OF FREE TRIALS

Another thing he said to avoid is free trials. Ultimately, in

disagree

121

these early phases, you're of course looking for money in sales, but it's more than that.

Bosmeny explained, "Your goal is to sign some deals, get some reference customers, get some validation, and get some revenue." In the case of free trials, you're not getting any of these things.

He usually responds to these requests with something like: "We don't do free trials. We do annual agreements and what we'll do is for the first 30 or 60 days, if for any reason you're not happy, you can opt out."

THE TAKE-AWAY

To conclude his talk, Bosmeny borrowed a lesson from Christoph Janz's blog post titled "The five ways to build a hundred million dollar company."

He said, through all of your sales, keep in mind if you're a company that needs a few big sales or a lot of small ones. This will be fundamental in prioritizing your time and attention in the areas where it matters most.

PART V

Fundraising

Raising money isn't the most important part of starting a startup. But — unless you're independently wealthy or can begin generating revenue right away — it's pretty hard to get much done without it.

These insights will turn you into a fundraising pro.

14

How to Raise Money

Featuring: Marc Andreessen, Ron Conway, and Parker Conrad

As a founder, raising venture capital is going to be one of the easiest things you do for your company. But, it's still no picnic.

Y Combinator president Sam Altman moderated a panel at Stanford University featuring three big names in startup fundraising to talk about everything from the big picture down to the nitty gritty details of asking people for money to support your next venture.

The panel included:

- **Marc Andreessen**: co-founder of Netscape; co-founder and General Partner at Andreessen Horowitz
- **Ron Conway:** a hero among angel investors and founder of SV Angel
- **Parker Conrad:** founder and CEO of Zenefits, a successful human resources startup

FUNDRAISING STAGES

When startups talk about fundraising, they're not talking about selling Girl Scout cookies.

Whether you're knocking on the door of Silicon Valley venture capital firms or amping up for Demo Day at a startup accelerator, raising money in the startup game comes in stages.

SEED STAGE

This is your initial capital used to conduct research, get patents, and generally get all the ducks in a row that you probably wouldn't have been able to without cash flow. This will help you build a strong foundation for the next stage.

SERIES A (AKA VENTURE)

With your product more streamlined and most of the company ownership still under your belt, this next phase will help you expand and hire a larger team.

SERIES B AND C (AKA SECOND AND THIRD STAGE)

This is a continuation of your startup financing and quest for external funds. With each round, you should be continuing to improve your product, and your pitch will follow.

After these stages, your road may take you to the bank, IPO, or acquisition, but that comes into play later. Right now, it's time to talk Series A.

HAVE A GOOD PRODUCT

Your product should be so good and self-sustaining that you don't even need to raise money.

After pitching to VC firms all up and down Silicon Valley, Conrad was given the advice to "be like the Twitter guys." That is to say, have a product so good that you don't even need a killer pitch. Your idea can initially sustain itself without all of the cash.

In fact, that's a trait that first attracted Conrad to the idea of Zenefits. And it turns out, that's an attractive trait to investors as well.

If you know your market so well that your product is lean, smart, and self-sufficient, then you've created something with momentum that's not dependent on cash. That's the kind of product confidence and direction that investors look for.

> As Andreessen put it, "You're always better off making your business better than you are making your pitch better."

The entire panel agreed that they look for the outliers — the ones whose ideas seem nuts at first (i.e. Airbnb), but they stand out as something "so crazy it just might work."

Crazy, but not without a plan, of course.

UNDERSTAND YOUR RISKS

Andreessen learned the "onion theory risk" from Andy Rachleff (co-founder and executive chairman of Wealthfront).

The idea is basically that, as a startup (especially before Seed funding), you are just layer upon layer of risk. Even after you get your first round of funding, it's not the money that makes those risks go away, it's what you do with it.

As you make smart decisions with your capital like finding a co-founder who's as good or better than you, conducting research, and gathering more data, you're achieving milestones in your business. And with each milestone, you're peeling away a layer of risk.

Because you're starting out with so much risk, early investors (Seed and Series A) are going to be more focused on attaining a percentage of ownership rather than something monetary. With that in mind, it's important to manage the amount of equity you're giving away, so that you don't end up with only a sliver of ownership for yourself.

Andreessen sees this as a big deterrent for investors in later stages because, for a founder with little stake in the company, the drive and ambition can quickly fizzle.

COVER YOUR BASES

Conway broke down some technical aspects of working with investors that are obvious, yet can be easily overlooked — especially by first-time entrepreneurs.

MASTER THE ONE-SENTENCE PITCH

You should be able to sum up your product in one sentence. This is not only good for refining your own vision, it's also a way to quickly and efficiently paint a picture of the product for an angel investor … or whoever is listening.

DON'T PROCRASTINATE

Things move fast in the startup world. In fact, every week Conway and the team at SV Angel look at about 30 companies and only invest in one on average.

Procrastinating (especially going into fundraising) can be a huge detriment when your cash competitors are going at full speed and staying nimble.

GET IT IN WRITING

After any important decision is made, you should send an email to the investor right away outlining what was discussed to make sure that both parties are on the same page. Conway said this small, simple step can eliminate a lot of potential controversy down the road.

THE TAKE-AWAY

Don't ever let funding determine a milestone or a starting point for your startup. In fact, the more you can do without it, the better.

If you can create a unique product with as little funding as possible, investors will be even more inclined to see what you can do with the additional resource of their money.

15

Perfecting Your Pitch

Featuring: Michael Seibel, Dalton Caldwell, and Qasar Younis

When it comes to fundraising, the devil truly is in the details — in this case, the investor meeting and your pitch.

Your early sales are not just going to involve selling your product. When you're trying to convince investors to give you money, you've got to know how to sell your big vision in a way that's clear, concise, and consistent.

A panel of three Y Combinator partners shared advice based on their own startup experiences about how to pitch your company and have a successful investor meeting.

KNOW YOUR PITCH

Michael Seibel is a Y Combinator partner who previously co-founded and served as CEO of Justin.tv and Socialcam.

In his time at these startups, he learned a lot about pitching, and the most important thing to remember is to always keep it short. He said that you really only need a 30-second pitch and a 2-minute pitch.

THE 30-SECOND PITCH

This how you talk about your company to people who are interested, even if not financially. You're not asking anything of them, but instead you're just explaining what it is your company does in three simple sentences.

1. What does your company do?

Seibel said, "You have to be able to [say this] in a way that is simple and straightforward ... You have to assume [the other person] knows nothing. Literally nothing about anything."

A good way to do this if you're a tech company is to pretend like you're talking to your mom or grandpa. If they can't understand in one sentence what your company does, you need to simplify more.

Seibel gave the example of Airbnb, saying that their sentence couldn't be "We're Airbnb and we're a marketplace for space." That means nothing. But, this does: "We're Airbnb and we allow you to rent out the extra room in your house."

2. How big is your market?

Find out what general industry you're in and how much it's worth. It's no mystery that people understand opportunity in terms of money, especially investors.

3. How much traction do you have?

This is where you talk about your growth rate and give some stats. Seibel said an example of this might be, "We launched in January and we're growing 30 percent month over month. We have this number of sales. This amount of revenue. This number of users."

Even if you're just getting started, it's important to emphasize how fast you're going. Whether you've been working for a few months or a year, this sentence needs to convince potential investors of your momentum.

THE 2-MINUTE PITCH

You've probably heard of the 10-minute pitch, but Seibel said that's a waste of time and that you can get it all done in two minutes, even when talking to investors.

> "One thing I like to tell founders is the more you talk, the more you have an opportunity to say something that people don't like. Talk less and it will probably be better."

So for your 2-minute pitch, start with the 30-second pitch, and then expand into these additional points, allowing a sentence for each.

1. What is your unique insight?

What are you bringing to the table that your competition isn't? What is your "secret sauce"?

Whatever you call it, this is the part where you want to tell the investor something you know that they don't know about your industry and your business. Their ideal expression should be kind of an ah-ha face.

This one can be two sentences, if necessary.

2. How do you make money?

Seibel said that founders can be weird about this point, especially if the answer is advertising. But it's best not to beat around the bush or sugarcoat because then it just seems like you have no idea how you're going to make money.

He said not to run away from this sentence. Speak simply and directly about how you plan to make money and then move on.

3. Who's on your team?

To investors, your co-founders' best achievements are going to be the ones that made other investors money, seeing as they want to make money too. Even if you don't have any of that on your founding team's résumé, do not resort to listing PhDs.

The investor wants to know how many founders you have

— Seibel said preferably between two and four. They also want to know how many are technical and how many are business-oriented.

Finally, be sure to mention how long you've known each other and how you met.

4. The Big Ask

Up until now, you've gone easy on the jargon, keeping things super simple and clear. But this is the part where that jargon comes in handy because it's important to talk about money in a way that's clear you understand it.

Seibel said that some of the things you should know are if you're raising on a safe or a convertible note, how much money you're raising, and what is the minimum check size.

And if you don't understand these terms, make Google your new best friend.

WHEN TO FUNDRAISE

Timing is key when talking to investors. Seibel said that you want to do it at a time when you're strong.

How do you know for sure that you're strong? He said, "If investors are asking to give you money, you're strong." If they aren't, you should be working more to get the word out about your brand.

Another way to show your strength is to build in a way

that you don't need their money to grow. The more self-sustaining your model is, the more you can show self-reliance and initiative, making investors even more certain that you'll handle their money efficiently.

Seibel said to give them the impression that this thing is moving with or without them. He also said that, if you do need money really early on, plan on needing less money and show traction and speed where you lack in age (of your company).

THE INVESTOR MEETING

So you've gotten an investor interested and they want to know more. From setting up the meeting to saying all the right things, the more flawless each step is the more likely they'll want to invest.

GET INTRODUCED

As with talking to the press, it's always best if you get introduced to potential investors through shared contacts. This helps your inquiry get to the top of the stack as it's already endorsed by someone they trust.

Keep in mind, though, that the credibility of the middle man (or woman) is super important. For example, if that person is an investor who's already passed on your company, Seibel said it's best not to use them as a connection.

MAKE A DATE

When it comes to scheduling the meetings, it's no time to drag things along. "It's a sprint. Not a marathon," Seibel said.

If possible, you want to schedule all of your investor meetings in the same week. If this sounds overwhelming, don't worry; Seibel has a nifty strategy.

To get all of your meetings on the same week, he likes to use a script like this: "Hey, we would love to set up a meeting but we're building like crazy for the next two weeks. So can we set it in that third week?"

This is far enough in the future that they have room in their schedule and you're able to get everyone in on the same week with enough time to prepare before then. It also gives the impression that you're not completely desperate for their money.

"It's signaling all of the right things," explained Seibel.

It's also best to have one person handling all of the investor scheduling as it can be really time consuming.

DOS AND DON'TS

Qasar Younis and Dalton Caldwell, both Y Combinator partners, finished off the lecture by sitting for a mock investor meeting and going over some final dos and don'ts of pitching your company and asking for money.

DO

- Let the person know exactly what you do. (See 30-second pitch above.)

- Teach the investor something, giving them some unique insight about your industry and your business.

- Move the conversation forward with confidence and clarity, which comes from knowing your facts.

- Ask for money. After all, that's what you're there for.

DON'T

- Make the meeting feel like a one-sided interview or an interrogation. It should feel more like a collaboration/ conversation.

- Meet with bad investors. Do research on who you're meeting with and find out if they're a good fit for your company.

- Let the conversation end when the meeting is over. Make sure you send follow-up correspondence.

- Fund until you're blue in the face. Fundraising is not the goal or a measure of success. It's what you do with the money that's important. So stop when you have what you need.

THE TAKE-AWAY

Funding is important but should not distract from or determine your success. If you know how to do it

properly, you can raise quickly and efficiently so you can afford to keep making progress with your company.

PART VI

Hiring

Early employees can make or break your startup. Here's what to look for in potential hires, plus advice on creating a solid company culture that reflects your values as the founder.

Solopreneur must
embody these traits

16

How to Hire the Best Team

Featuring: Sam Altman

According to Sam Altman, your ideal co-founder is James Bond. But if you're not that lucky, you should know what qualities to look for in startup teammates.

Altman, the president of Y Combinator, doesn't mean your startup should be filled with trigger-happy philanderers who spend their free time getting wasted.

But, like James Bond, a great co-founder is unflappable, tough, and knows what to do in every situation. He or she needs to act quickly and be decisive, creative, and ready for anything.

As the leader of a team, you need to have some Bond in yourself, too — but don't worry, the tuxedo is optional.

CO-FOUNDER RELATIONSHIPS ARE CRITICAL

Altman said that co-founder relationships are among the most important in the entire company.

"You have to watch out for tension brewing among co-founders and you have to address it immediately," he said.

> *"The number one cause of early death for startups is co-founder blowups. But for some reason, a lot of people treat choosing their co-founder with even less importance than hiring. Don't do this!"*

Instead, make sure you're looking for someone whose skills complement your own and who can fill in the gaps that you can't. Also, look for someone with those Bond qualities.

HAVING A LOT OF EMPLOYEES DOESN'T MEAN YOU'RE COOL

Of course, after you find a co-founder, you'll probably want to start hiring employees. But Altman cautioned founders to resist the urge to hire people right away.

A startup that has many employees may seem cool, but careful hiring in the early stages is key for the longevity of your startup. Only hire when the workload is too much for your existing team.

Unfortunately, the cost of getting an early hire wrong is

really high. In fact, Altman said one bad hire can kill a young startup.

Building an effective team takes time and thought. And without a really good team, it will be harder to execute on your ideas and grow your startup. So don't rush the process.

LEARNING FROM AIRBNB

Five months. That's how long Y Combinator alum Airbnb spent interviewing their first employee. And they only hired two employees their first year.

Before hiring anyone, the founders wrote down a list of the values that they wanted every Airbnb employee to have. The most important value? Candidates had to "bleed" Airbnb. If they didn't, they wouldn't get hired.

For example, Airbnb CEO Brian Chesky used to ask people if they would take the job even if they had only one year left to live. That question alone was enough to weed out the people who didn't really possess the values Airbnb was looking for.

Your employees play a huge part in defining your company. That's why you need to hire people who believe in your startup as much as you do.

HIRING AMAZING PEOPLE

Altman said, "The best source for hiring by far is people that you already know and people that other employees in the company already know."

Experience is not always a reliable factor. Experience matters when you're hiring someone to manage a large part of your organization. But for your early hires, consider their aptitude and their belief in your mission instead.

THE IMPORTANCE OF PROJECTS

Startups don't operate like traditional businesses, so why hire like one?

Altman recommended having the candidate work on a project in lieu of an interview. But if you've decided on conducting traditional interviews, then you should at least ask about projects that people have worked on in the past.

REFERENCE CHECK

Altman also proposed contacting their references and asking questions like:

- Is this person in the top 5% of people you've ever worked with?
- What specifically did they do?
- Would you hire them again?
- Why aren't you trying to hire them again?

ATTRIBUTES OF AN IDEAL CANDIDATE

Here are some of the key qualities to look for in a potential hire:

- Good communication skills

- Risk-taking attitude

- Maniacally determined

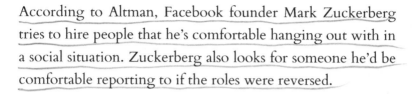

According to Altman, Facebook founder Mark Zuckerberg tries to hire people that he's comfortable hanging out with in a social situation. Zuckerberg also looks for someone he'd be comfortable reporting to if the roles were reversed.

It's important that you enjoy working with your employees. Your team doesn't need matching BFF necklaces, but nothing is worse than resenting someone with whom you spend 40-60 hours a week.

When it comes to attracting and maintaining talent, it doesn't hurt to offer generous equity.

It's better to give your employees more equity than your investors, because employees will only add more value over time. According to Altman, Y Combinator companies that have done this well are often the most successful.

RETAINING YOUR EMPLOYEES

Of course, your work is not done after you hire your employees; now you need to retain them. And that can actually involve more work than the hiring process.

With retention, the goal is to ensure that your employees are happy and feel valued. That means that first-time CEOs need to learn management skills.

According to Altman, a speaker at a Y Combinator event told other startup founders how he learned from his failings as a CEO. Even though he's successful now, he had a hard time holding on to his employees early on in his startup.

Someone asked him what his biggest struggle was and he said: "Turns out you shouldn't tell your employees they're fucking up every day unless you want them all to leave because they will."

QUALITIES OF A GREAT CEO

As a CEO, you have to be aware that, by default, you're going to be a bad manager.

You need to overcompensate for that with these tips, which come down to giving employees autonomy, mastery, and purpose. Famed business author Dan Pink said those are great motivators to get people to do great work.

Let your team take credit for all the good stuff. You need to take responsibility for the bad stuff.

Don't micromanage. Let people have small areas of responsibility. This will actually push them to work harder.

FIRING PEOPLE WHEN IT'S NOT WORKING

Altman said there are three things to ask yourself about a potential hire. If the answer to all three is "yes," then chances are you won't regret your hire.

1. Are they smart?
2. Do they get things done?
3. Do I want to spend a lot of time around them?

Unfortunately, though, for one reason (or many) things won't work out sometimes. Despite taking all the care in the world during the hiring process, sometimes you need to fire people.

If you're hesitant about firing someone, it helps to evaluate his performance. Most people will mess up a few times. But if a person always does the opposite of what you would have done in a given situation, then you need to let him go.

If it's not working out with one of your employees but you don't want to fire him, then maybe you just need to move him into a new position. It helps to hire smart people who are great at learning new things. Those kinds of people will fit pretty much anywhere you put them.

EXECUTION MAKES ALL THE DIFFERENCE

Execution is one of those founder tasks that you can't outsource. Ideas are worth nothing without execution.

If you look at a company that executes well, chances are its CEO is a master executor. So if you want a culture where people work hard, pay attention to detail, and manage the customers, you have to represent those qualities as a leader.

Whatever the founders do becomes the culture.

A CEO's job is often categorized as having four components – see the vision, raise money, evangelize the mission to people you're trying to recruit, and hire and manage the team. But Altman said that there's a fifth component: setting the execution bar.

He said, "Execution gets divided into two key questions. One: Can you figure out what to do? And two: Can you get it done?"

KEYS TO MASTERING EXECUTION

1. What you're spending your time and your money on reveals what you, as a founder, think is important. Identifying the two or three things you need to focus on each day will help you to execute better.

2. Say "no" to almost everything. You need to focus your attention on the right things.

3. Be intense. Running a startup will consume your life, leaving little chance for true work-life balance. You need to outwork your competitors and that means countless long nights, at least in the beginning.

The enemy of execution is indecisiveness.

> *"Indecisiveness is a startup killer. Mediocre founders spend a lot of time talking about grand plans, but they never make a decision."*

The power of decisive action is something Altman knows about first-hand.

His company was about to lose out on a deal with an important client, so he called the potential customer and told them that his product was better and tried to set up a meeting with them. They told Altman that they were signing the deal with his competitor and nothing could change their minds.

Instead of accepting defeat, Altman and his team got on a plane and arrived at the potential client's office at 6 a.m. They ended up ripping up the contract with the other company and Altman's startup closed the deal with them a week later.

Had they not gotten on a plane and shown up in person, they would've missed out on a valuable customer.

GROWTH AND MOMENTUM FUEL STARTUPS

Startups must never lose focus on growth and momentum. That's why intensity is a requirement for any successful startup. Unlike traditional companies, startups are working to move fast while also being obsessed with quality.

"Momentum and growth are the lifeblood of startups," said Altman.

"You want a company to be winning all the time. If you ever take your foot off the gas pedal, things will spiral out of control. A team that hasn't won in a while gets demotivated and keeps losing. So always keep momentum."

For most software startups, this means they need to keep

growing. For hardware startups, this means that they can't let their ship dates slip.

In 2008, Facebook's growth was slowing down and so was their morale. Zuckerberg responded to this burgeoning crisis by creating a growth group to work on small projects.

This group lived up to its name and got Facebook back on track. Morale improved and now the growth group is the most innovative part of the Facebook family.

HOW TO KEEP MOMENTUM

Maintain momentum by establishing an operating rhythm at the company early on. This means shipping products and launching new features on a regular basis and reviewing metrics every week with the entire company.

This is where your Board of Directors can come in handy. They often get companies to care about metrics and milestones.

THE TAKE-AWAY

When you need to hire a team, the process shouldn't be rushed. Everyone on your team has to have the passion and initiative that you have in order to make your business a success.

17

Creating Company Culture

Featuring: Alfred Lin

At Zappos, the company culture is so closely tied to their values that they'll pay you to leave if you don't fit the bill.

The online clothing and shoe shop takes hiring very seriously. Every person the company hires, no matter what department they're in, goes through a four-week training program.

New hires answer phone calls from Zappos' customers for the first two weeks. But it's after the first week that Zappos offers to pay people for the training with an additional $2,000 bonus if they quit right on the spot.

It may seem like a ludicrous way to operate a company, but it's effective at weeding out the people who are just in it for the money.

As Zappos' number two in command for five years, Alfred Lin brought the online retailer to its first profitable year in 2006 and was integral to its $1.2 billion acquisition.

TechCrunch said Lin has the Midas touch, because every company he's ever worked for has been acquired, with the smallest deal amounting to $265 million.

Now he's a partner at venture capital firm Sequoia Capital. And it seems that maybe his startup gold has a lot to do with creating an ideal company culture.

HOW TO DEFINE CULTURE

Lin said that the real question is what the company culture is going to be. You can figure it out with his fill-in-the-blank formula.

In its most basic form, company culture can be defined as _____1_____ member of the team in pursuit of a company's _____2_____.

Blank #1: Your company's assumptions, beliefs, and values

Blank #2: An action

WHY DOES CULTURE MATTER?

It's impossible to pursue your company's destiny if you don't have a good culture.

Once you define your company culture, you'll always be using it as a guide for business decisions. This provides you with "stability to fall back on" because "it becomes a way to align people on values that matter to the company," Lin said.

When explaining why culture matters, Lin also quoted Gandhi:

> *"Your beliefs become your thoughts. Your thoughts become your words. Your words become your actions. Your actions become the habits. Your habits become your values. And your values become your destiny."*

A CLEARLY-DEFINED COMPANY CULTURE PROVIDES THREE THINGS:

1. **Trust.** People like to know what type of company they're committing to. And, as a founder, you're trusting that you made good hiring decisions because your team shares your values.
2. **Guidance.** It'll help you figure out what to do and what not to do.
3. **Support.** It'll help you know which employees to retain.

In a popular Medium post, Airbnb CEO Brian Chesky pinpointed why culture is so important to him as a founder.

"The stronger the culture, the less corporate process a company needs," wrote Chesky.

"When the culture is strong, you can trust everyone to do the right thing. People can be independent and autonomous. They can be entrepreneurial. And if we have a company that is entrepreneurial in spirit, we will be able to take our next '(wo)man on the moon' leap."

"Ever notice how families or tribes don't require much process?", he continued. "That is because there is such a strong trust and culture that it supersedes any process. In organizations (or even in a society) where culture is weak, you need an abundance of heavy, precise rules and processes."

Not every hire is going to be a good fit. There's no way around that. But the benefit of a strong company culture is that it makes it that much easier to weed out the bad hires from the good. Being able to know who to keep and who to let go right away will save your company.

CREATING YOUR CULTURE

A company's culture begins with the founding team and leaders of the company. The definition of that culture is based on the values of those people.

GETTING STARTED

Lin advises that you ask yourself these questions to determine the direction of your company's culture:

1. What are the values that are most important to you? Of those, which are most important to the business?
2. What are the types of people you like working with? And what are their values?
3. Now think about all the people that you've never liked working with. What values do they have? Think of the opposite of that; maybe those should be considered values for your company, too.

It's important to keep in mind that the values must align with your company mission and be uniquely tied to that mission.

Lin said that, at Zappos, their big culture focus was on customer service, so their top priority was to create that "wow" experience for customers. Their second priority was to serve.

NARROWING YOUR FOCUS

If your list of core values is looking a little long, that's not a bad thing. When Zappos began the process of identifying their core values, they listed 37. It took a year to get the list down to 10.

It might seem odd that it took them so long, but Lin says there's an important reason why it took a year to really define their culture:

"[If] you just come up with the word honesty. Give me a break, everybody wants the culture to be honest. Nobody is going to say: 'I want to be lied to every day.' What do you mean by 'service'? There's got to be a lot more depth in this than that. And everybody talks about 'teamwork.' How do you dive deeper into 'teamwork'? What are the things that don't work for a team?"

It's easy to say that you want to be this and do that. But actually investigating what that means and what it looks like is an entirely different story. Delving deeper into the connotations of those values takes time, effort, and patience.

WHY DO TEAMS FAIL?

In *The Five Dysfunctions of a Team,* author Patrick Lencioni deconstructed why teams fall apart.

Team dysfunction happens because of a lack of trust and a fear of commitment. If people move past their fear of commitment, then the next thing that goes wrong is a lack of accountability. Without that accountability, you won't get any results.

If you're taking team performance into consideration (and you should), then you'll need to spend more time ruminating on your company's values. Lin thinks it's a big no-no when companies don't interview for culture fit.

He said, "You can have the smartest engineer in the world but if they don't believe the mission, they are not going to pour their heart and soul into it. [You need to think] about culture – from the interview process, to performance reviews, to making sure that [it's] a daily habit. You get a lot further with making a great culture."

Think of all the things you want your company to do. What's keeping you from reaching those goals? Come up with solutions to those problems and make them part of your company culture daily habit.

It's like fitness. Wishing to be in shape won't make it happen (though that would be awesome). You have to make it part of your routine every day.

If you don't make fitness a daily habit, what happens? You can't do all of the things you'd built up the skill and endurance to do. The same goes for your company habits.

THE TAKE-AWAY

Once you have a clear definition of your company culture, you need to make it the cornerstone of your business decisions, especially hiring. Everything works better when everyone is working toward the same goal and operating by the same set of values.

18

Advice on Hiring and Culture from the Founders of Pinterest and Stripe

Featuring: Ben Silbermann, John Collison, and Patrick Collison

Team building is not all forest retreats and happy hours. It's an exercise in building a better company every single day.

As a follow-up to Alfred Lin's lecture on company culture, Sam Altman asked a trio of prominent founders about the problems that arise when building an early team and how to maintain the culture they've worked so hard to develop as their companies grow.

The panel at Stanford University featured Ben Silbermann, co-founder of Pinterest, and brothers John and Patrick Collison, co-founders of Stripe.

Editor's Note: Questions and responses have been edited for length. The speaker's initials precede his comments below.

WHAT ARE THE CORE PIECES OF CULTURE THAT YOU FOUND TO BE MOST IMPORTANT IN BUILDING OUT YOUR COMPANIES?

BS: For us, we think on a few dimensions: One is who we hire – what those people value. Two is what we do every day. Why do we do it? Three is what we choose to communicate, and I think four is how we choose to celebrate. Then the converse of this is what you choose to punish. But, in general, I think running a company based on what we celebrate is more exciting than what we punish.

JC: I think [what] Stripe has placed a large emphasis on, more so than other companies, is transparency, internally. I think it's something that's been really valuable for Stripe, and a little bit misunderstood. If everyone really believes in the mission, that if everyone has really good access to information and everyone has a good picture of the current state of Stripe, then that gets you a huge amount of the way there in terms of working productively together. And it forgives a lot of the other things that tend to break as you grow a startup.

WHAT DID YOU LOOK FOR WHEN HIRING YOUR FIRST 10 EMPLOYEES TO GET THE CULTURE OF THE COMPANY RIGHT?

BS: Clearly I looked for people that I wanted to work with and I thought were talented. When we first hired people, we hired people that were more like ourselves. I often looked for three to four things that I really valued in people: I looked for people who worked hard, had high integrity, and a low ego. I looked for people who were creative, super curious, which meant they had all of these interests.

One guy made his own board game, with his own elaborate set of rules. Another guy was really into magic tricks. He not only coded a magic trick on an iPhone, but he shot the production video in the preview. We really want someone who wants to build something great. And they aren't arrogant about it, but they want to take a risk and build something bigger than themselves.

JC: The first 10 hires is really hard, because you're making these first 10 hires at a point where no one's heard of this company before. Nobody wants to work with you.

No batch of 10 people will have as big of an influence on the company as those first 10 people.

For us, it was over a very long time period talking to people we knew, or friends of friends into joining. We didn't have huge networks. We were both still in college back then. So there were really no people that we worked with to draw in.

So a lot of those early Stripers were people we heard of from friends. The other interesting thing they had in common: they were all really early in their career or undervalued in some way.

PC: You have to think like a value investor. You're looking for the human capital that's significantly valued by the market. You probably shouldn't look to hire your friends from Facebook and Google, or whatever. They are already discovered. They are probably harder to convince.

For our first 10 people, [we wanted people who were] also very genuine and straight. That they are intellectually honest [with] how they approach problems. They are generally people who like to get things finished. There are a lot of people who are really excited about tons of things. Only some of those are excited about completing things. And then the third trait that we looked for is that they cared a great deal. It's offensive to them when something is just a little off.

HOW DID YOU FIND THEM?

BS: I don't think there is a wrong place to find people. So when I look back at our first hires … they came from all over the place. I put up ads on Craigslist. I went to random TED Talks. We used to throw weekly BBQs at the office [where] we would just talk to folks.

But I think the really good people are doing something

else, so you have to go seek them out instead of expecting that they are going to seek you out.

JC: Have a great elevator pitch, not just for investors but because everyone that you run into right now is six months to a year down the road [to being a] recruit. So the right time to have gotten them excited about your product, the right time for them to have started following us, is as soon as it can start. It's going to take a very long time to recruit people, so getting people consistently excited about what you are doing will pay back later.

AS A RELATIVELY INEXPERIENCED FOUNDER, HOW DO YOU IDENTIFY WHO THE REALLY GOOD PEOPLE ARE?

BS: You will never 100% know until you work with folks. Before we talk to anyone, we try to figure out what exactly is world class in that discipline. So I always made it a habit of mine to talk to people I knew de facto were world class and just asking them, what are the traits you look for? What are the questions you ask? And how to find them?

The other thing the questions are supposed to do is give us a sense of: "Is this the right place for this person to come in and work?" This is the point you guys made about being very transparent.

When they were recruiting for iPhone, they didn't even tell people what they were doing. You won't see your families for three years, but when you are done, your kids, your kids'

kids will remember what you built. I think that's a really good thing in recruiting as well. Be very, very transparent on why you think it's a great idea, but you lay out in gory detail why it's going to be hard. And then the right people select in or they select out of that opportunity.

PC: I think a specific tactical thing to do, again for the first 10 people, is to work with them as much as you can before committing to hire them. Once you hit a certain scale, it's kind of impractical to put them on that side and be unskilled.

Another answer I thought of to the question "How do you know if someone if great?": Is this person the best out of all of their friends at what they do? A better way to think about it is, "Is this the best engineer this engineer knows?"

BS: I think referencing people is really important. Referencing people is just what it sounds like – asking people with experience for their honest opinion. We are trying not to validate if they told the truth on their resumes because we assume they told the truth.

I typically ask something that makes the question … feel a little bit more quantitative and then calibrate that over time. To evaluate this person's dimensions, is this person the top 1% of the people you worked with, the top 5%, the top 10%? And it forces scarcity that gives them material reference.

HOW DO YOU MAKE NEW EMPLOYEES EFFECTIVE

QUICKLY AND GET THEM TO THE RIGHT CULTURE PLACE?

BS: We spend a lot of time thinking and constantly trying to refine what that person looked like from the day they came in, to their first interview, through 30 days after they joined. Do they [know] someone's name? Do they know who their manager is? Have they sat down [with] people on their team? Do they know what the general arch of the company is? And what the top priorities are? Then we also ask their peers and manager, 'Hey is this person up to speed? Do you feel we did a good job at making them productive?'

If we haven't, then that's a key that a) we should not be hiring any more people because we're not doing a good job bringing in new people and b) we need to retool.

I think those things are important. I just wouldn't discount how important it is to get to know the person as a person. What are their aspirations? What's their working style? How do they like to be recognized? Do they really prefer being in total silence? Are they a morning person or night person? Knowing those things demonstrates that you care about them individually and collectively.

JC: I think there are two things that are important at any stage:

First is to get them up and running quickly to do the work. That is how you are going to find the problems, it is how progress is measured in the real work they are doing. And so when we have engineers start, we try to get them committing (code) on the first day. When we have people in business roles start, we will have them in real meetings the first day on what they are meant to be working on.

Then second, we try to quickly give people feedback. Expectedly, giving people feedback on how you adapt to the culture. When you think about it, if you have built a strong culture as all the companies up here are trying to, it's going to take some adapting from the person. One thing we have at Stripe is the culture is a lot more written. So you have people next to each other, with headphones on, IMing each other. And for a lot of people coming in and working in an environment like that it's sort of hard —

PC: [Coming] in from normal places.

JC: Exactly, yeah. **So from everything high level of how you are doing at your job to minor cultural issues, the more feedback you give them, the better they will do.**

WHAT ARE THE BIGGEST CHANGES YOU'VE HAD TO MAKE AS YOU TRANSITIONED FROM 10 TO 100 TO 1,000 EMPLOYEES?

PC: In the early days, you have to hire people who are going to be productive. Essentially, you don't have the luxury of hiring people [who] look to be promising, but they are not going to be up to speed for another year or two. They have to be able to work immediately. But after two or three years, then it becomes much more reasonable to make those investments.

HAVE THE PEOPLE YOU HIRED EARLY BEEN ABLE TO GROW INTO LEADERSHIP ROLES?

JC: In Stripe's case, yes. A lot of the first 10 people are in leadership roles now. People don't exactly come out of the womb being good at management or at leadership. And being able to develop that in people and helping people progress as they spend a number of years at the company [is important]. It's a lot of work when people are running around with their hair on fire. But it's also damaging if the company can't develop that skill.

BS: I think for us, the answer is some yes and some no. **I think one of the benefits of working at a startup is you can be handed a challenge no one else would be crazy enough to let you take on.** And that could be managing people. It could be taking on a project.

And also if you ask someone to take a risk like that, it shouldn't be one way through the door if you don't succeed. Otherwise it creates fear to give it a shot. So we have some folks managing a large team at the start, individual programmers, individual engineers. And they say, "Hey I would love to try leading a project, leading a group," then taking responsibility for management.

Then we have other folks that try it and are really glad they did so they know they never want to do that again. We try that. For those people, you can have just as much impact on the company through your individual contributions as an engineer or what have you. But it's really hard to predict unless you give people a shot. So my strong preference is you give as many people a shot as possible.

And in the few areas where you feel there is too much of a learning curve relative to the business development you are trying to achieve, that is when you look for someone who might walk in and really execute well on the job.

HOW DO YOU CONVINCE PEOPLE TO MAKE SACRIFICES TO JOIN A STARTUP?

PC: I think part of why it resonates with people is because it's not guaranteed. If it was, it would be boring.

There is the prospect of affecting this outcome, but nothing more than that potential. As far as not seeing their families and kids, startups do involve longer hours in the beginning, but I think that story is overstated. Even the startups that in the earlier days had some sort of longer working days have a tendency to exaggerate. It's kind of like the startup version of fishing.

I think realistically for most people, it's not that big of a sacrifice. I think, on average, people work two hours more a day. It is a sacrifice, but it is not forgoing all pleasure and enjoyment for the next half decade.

BS: Even the iPhone wasn't the iPhone before it got done. No smart person you are hiring thinks you have a crystal ball into the future that only you have and that joining is a guaranteed thing. And, in fact, if you are telling them that and they select in, maybe you shouldn't be hiring them because they didn't pass a basic intelligence test of certainty and the future.

But I think it's fair to say what's exciting and where you think you can go. And where it's going to be hard and chart your best plan. And then tell them why their role in it can be instrumental because it is.

If people are joining because they want all the certainty of Google and the perks of working in a small startup with more email transparency, then that's a really negative sign. For example, when I interview people, they often say, "I'm really passionate about what you are doing." I often ask where else they are interviewing.

If they list seven companies that have nothing to do with each other, except they are at the same stage, "I love the stage of discovery, so I'm interviewing at Stripe, Jawbone, Airbnb, Uber, I'm also putting my resume into Google X," that's a sign they are probably not being authentic, which you care about. And those folks, when things get hard, they won't stick it out and work through it, because they were really signing up for an experience, not for achieving a goal.

HOW DOES YOUR USER BASE AFFECT YOUR HIRING STRATEGY?

BS: You only hire people who use your product religiously every day. For us, we screen for people who have vision and discovery online. And they have to know how our service works, and they have to have used it.

But they may not be a lifelong user, and for us that's great. We can ask: what is the barrier that is preventing you from using it? Come join, we will move that barrier. Help us get closer to that vision.

JC: Hiring people who are passionate about your product is a great way to find people.

You have a natural advantage over other companies. I know in Stripe's case, we hired four Stripe users, people who we probably couldn't have gotten otherwise. I'm sure it was the same in Pinterest's case.

THE TAKE-AWAY

As you start to build a team, focus on interviewing potential hires based on their intentions and their work ethic. Be honest and transparent about your vision of the company and expect the same from them.

Your early hires will be the most important, so make sure that you know the must-ask questions to avoid any missteps.

PART VII

Scaling

After building your product and attracting an initial user base, it's time to focus on growth. Here's advice on the best way to scale from folks who've learned these lessons first-hand.

19

Doing Things That Don't Scale

Featuring: Stanley Tang and Walker Williams

When you're starting a startup, your big ideas can get in the way of taking the important initial baby steps.

Stanley Tang of DoorDash set out to discover how to make technology that could help solve problems for small businesses. Turns out, a big problem for small business is establishing a delivery infrastructure.

So, Stanley and his future co-founders put together a super touch-and-go website with a few menus for people in Palo Alto, CA to order food from a variety of local restaurants.

The idea gained traction. And, after many conversations with local business owners and only an hour of site-building, DoorDash was launched with a simple website and the founders as the delivery people.

Walker Williams, Teespring founder and CEO, also operated from this school of thought. His company allows people to launch product and apparel brands without risk, cost, or compromise. In his early stages, he found that listening to customers was as pivotal as acting quickly on the insights he gained.

By abiding by the idea of "doing things that don't scale," these founders were able to harness the control and energy of a small startup team that doesn't need to have all of the answers at the beginning.

It's a process of using the resources you have to accomplish what you need at the moment and then using those efficient solutions you build early on as a foundation for success.

Sometimes the best way to see if something works, and to see if people will love it, is to just put it out there with the minimal resources you have.

As Tang put it, "We just launched because at the beginning it's all about testing the idea, trying to get this thing off the ground, and figuring out if this was something people even wanted. And it's okay to hack things together at the beginning."

Straight from their own experiences, Tang and Williams offered advice to other founders on how to hit the ground running.

TREAT YOUR STARTUP LIKE AN EXPERIMENT

You're probably really attached to your big idea, and that's great. But as with most ideas, when it leaves your head and gets some air you might find that it doesn't ignite with everyone in the way that you were hoping.

That's probably because not everyone is like you, which is okay. In order to "roll with the punches," you've got to stay flexible, nimble, and open to potential changes you see for your company, so you can continue to learn and grow right into product-market fit.

Williams strongly believes in turning your users into champions with a memorable, delightful experience. This is how you'll continue to test your hypothesis (aka your big idea).

Even if someone has left your service with a negative experience, he said that you should always do everything you can to make it right. As many restaurants on Yelp would attest, it only takes one dissatisfied user to taint your entire image online.

Williams said that, no matter what goes wrong, "You just have to bite the bullet and make sure it's right. And the customers who are originally the most frustrated tend to turn into the biggest champions and the longest-term users."

When you make it clear in your head that nothing is set in stone, then when you're getting that invaluable feedback from your users — good or bad — you'll be able to hear it with a more open mind. Moreover, you'll be amped to improve the experience for them and future users.

Williams added, "The quicker you talk to users and learn what they actually need, the faster you can get to [scale]."

SHORT-TERM SOLUTIONS LEAD TO LONG-TERM SOLUTIONS

DoorDash's small startup team pieced together tools they already knew how to use to assemble a makeshift system that worked for them in those early stages: Square to receive payments, a Google Doc to track orders, and Apple's Find My Friends to keep track of their drivers.

In the beginning, that's all okay. With a small team, small mistakes are just that. But with a big team and a lot of (wo)manpower, small mistakes have a bigger impact. So it's good to weed out as many mistakes as possible in the beginning to find solutions that really work best.

Even as you continue to build on these short-term solutions and begin turning them into more permanent systems, scaling shouldn't be your ultimate goal.

 "The lesson that I've been learning lately is that you want to do things

that don't scale as long as possible," said Williams. "It's one of your biggest advantages as a company, and the moment you give it up, you're giving your competitors that are smaller and can still do these things that advantage over you."

BECOME AN EXPERT IN EVERY ASPECT OF YOUR BUSINESS

When you're the founder/operations department/customer support, you really get to see how the ins and outs of your business flow ... or don't. With a strong base and a complete understanding of your customers, you can gradually make solutions for your company that are more intentional and less experimental.

While launching Teespring, Williams found that it was invaluable for the founders to do whatever it took to bring in users themselves. This means putting in a lot of extra time with those early customers. "Do not expect to spend an hour and return thousands of dollars," he said.

"For most of us, those first two users are going to take a lot of handholding, a lot of personal love, and that's okay — that's essential for building a company."

It's important to note that just because you're taking small steps doesn't mean that you're moving slowly. In fact, quite the opposite.

As you continue to learn more and more about your business and get a system in place, it's important that you move fast because the market is moving fast. If you get stuck and dwell on one thing, the market won't wait for you.

FINDING PRODUCT-MARKET FIT

The biggest perk of doing things that don't scale is that you can continue learning and adapting until you find your perfect little niche — the little hole that your company has been built to fill.

So, especially in the early days of your business, Walker said it's important to keep in mind that "the product you launch with will almost certainly not be the product that takes you to scale. So your job in those early days of a startup is to progress and iterate as fast as possible to reach that product that does have market fit."

The smaller and more nimble you are, the faster you'll be able to get closer to that next point of scale and eventually finding your market fit.

To keep your eyes on what's attainable, Williams said to "only worry about the next order of magnitude ... [So] when you have your tenth user, you shouldn't be wondering how you are going to serve one million users."

If you look at these short-term goals as bread crumbs, they'll lead you right where you need to be.

THE TAKE-AWAY

The biggest takeaway of these startups' early success

stories is to start small, hit the ground running, and don't slow down until you're truly prepared to scale.

This process will test your tenacity, your patience, and even your dedication. But if you stay light on your feet, listen to your users, and don't stop until they're satisfied, you'll have the foundation of a sustainable business model and the experience to keep growing with confidence.

20

3 Essentials for Scaling

Featuring: Adora Cheung

When the founders of Homejoy wanted to disrupt the cleaning industry, they learned how to scale (and clean) from scratch.

When Adora Cheung and her brother Aaron had the idea to shake up the antiquated cleaning industry, they took a novel approach – they became a part of the cleaning industry.

Right away they realized that they were bad cleaners, so they started buying books on the topic. But reading books wasn't enough to get the training they needed, so they got a job at a cleaning company.

This became a valuable experience because, not only did they learn how a local cleaning company works, but they were able to locate the inefficiencies within the system and then build Homejoy to solve those problems.

Here are the three essential for scaling that Cheung discussed in a lecture at Stanford:

1. BUILDING YOUR PRODUCT

DETERMINE YOUR FEATURES

Before you build your product, the first thing you need to do is ask yourself, **"What is the smallest feature set that I should build to solve the problem that I'm trying to solve?"**

Cheung suggested answering that question by talking to users, seeing what already exists, and building to solve your users' immediate needs.

POSITION YOUR PRODUCT

The second thing you need to do is establish your product positioning. That's something that took Homejoy a long time to learn.

"When we went to potential users to come on our platform they would kind of get bored after the first few sentences. What we found out was that we needed a one-liner. The one-liner was very important. It kind of describes the functional benefits of what you do," Cheung said.

"After we changed our position to 'Get your place cleaned for $20 an hour,' then everyone got it, and we were able to get users in the door that way."

2. GETTING USERS TO TRY YOUR PRODUCT

Once they were able to simplify their message, the Homejoy team could focus on getting users to try their product.

They actually had a very hard time getting people to sign up initially, so they had to use unconventional methods like handing out water bottles at a street fair on a hot day.

"We started handing out free bottles of water that were cold. And people just came to us. I think we basically guilt-tripped people into booking cleanings. But the proof in the pudding was that I figured most of the people were guilt tripped into doing it, but then they went home and they didn't cancel on us."

At that point, they had users and wanted to be able to get as much feedback as possible. According to Cheung, getting user feedback requires these tenets:

- **Always have a way for people to contact you.** Homejoy used a phone number and voicemail.

- **Visiting users and talking to them works best.**

- **Make it a conversation.** Make sure you're not interrogating the users you talk to. Instead, get to know them and make them feel comfortable by framing it as a conversation. Cheung recommended taking people out for drinks or coffee.

3. GROWING USERS

When it comes to scaling your startup, the aim is to get a good return on the money you're investing.

You want a growth model that is sustainable. But to foster sustainable growth, you need to understand the three types of growth: sticky, viral, and paid.

STICKY GROWTH

With this kind of growth, your main goal is to secure returning users. Cheung said that the key to sticky growth is providing a great experience.

The better the customer experience, the more people will want to use your product. You want to be so addictive that people are compelled to use your product.

VIRAL GROWTH

Like its name suggests, this type of growth is what happens when people talk about you. Viral growth depends on a solid referral program, which is made up of three main parts:

1. Awareness

Where are people learning that they can refer other people? Cheung advises offering a sign-up after they use the product.

2. Platform-Type Play

When the cleaning professional is inside a user's home, they can give the user a card that points them to a link for referrals.

3. Program Mechanics

An example of this would be getting $10 if you invite your friends. Then they use it, and they get $10 as well.

PAID GROWTH

When you have money to spend, then paid growth is a viable option. The key is that your customer's lifetime value (CLV) needs to be more than your customer acquisition costs (CAC).

Let's say you begin running a bunch of ads over the course of 12 months, but the conversion rates are different for each one. And there are different acquisition costs for different types of ads.

Figuring out whether each ad is successful or not means subtracting the CAC from the CLV. If it is more than zero, then you are earning a profit.

DON'T BE AFRAID TO PIVOT

Homejoy achieved a lot of success, but Cheung said that it was the 13th idea that they built, executed, and onboarded users for. Determining which idea is the "Golden One" requires long-term thinking.

"Once you realize that you can't grow, and despite building out all of these great features and talking to all of these users none of them stick, or the economics of the business just don't make sense – then once you make that realization you just need to move on," she said.

THE TAKE-AWAY

Cheung emphasized the need for a growth plan from the very beginning. Ask yourself: What is an optimistic but realistic way to grow this business? Then, with the long-term in mind, you can dive in.

21

Lessons from Facebook's VP of Growth

Featuring: Alex Schultz

When it comes to growth, there are many important factors to consider. But Facebook's top growth executive says the most important one is retention.

Since 2007, Alex Schultz has worked as the VP of Growth at Facebook. But it turns out that he fell into it accidentally by way of physics.

Like many origin stories, Schultz's interest in marketing was driven by a lack of money. Specifically, he got into online marketing because he needed to pay for college.

By the 1990s, he became fascinated by the world of SEO back when "it was a really, really easy skill to learn."

He learned to program because he was tired of being the nerdiest person in physics class and taught himself the skill through the creation of a cocktail-making site — it became the largest cocktail site in the UK.

Then he fell into growth hacking before it even had a real name. In his mind, it was just Internet marketing: "Using whatever channel you can to get whatever output you want."

Schultz not only paid for college with his online marketing work, he ended up deciding to leave physics behind and focus on marketing for his career.

PAY ATTENTION TO YOUR RETENTION CURVE

What do you think matters most for growth? Great products, customers, or word of mouth? It's actually the combination of all three: retention.

It's a given that startups want to grow, so Schultz contended that the most important graph that any founder can look at is a retention curve.

If you plot the percentage of monthly active users versus the number of days from acquisition, you should end up with a retention curve that is asymptotic to a line parallel to the X-axis. That's when you have a viable business.

Schultz explained that your next step is to see how many of your users have been using your product for one day. Ask yourself: What percentage of them are active monthly?

"100% for the first 30 days obviously, because monthly active, they also end up on one day," he said. "But then you look at 31. Every single user on their 31st day after registration, what percentage of them are monthly active? Thirty-second day, thirty-third day, thirty-fourth day."

Even if you only have 10,000 customers, you're still going to get an idea of what this curve is going to look like for your product. You're going to be able to tell if it's asymptotic.

"If it doesn't flatten out, don't go into growth tactics. Don't do virality. Don't hire a growth hacker. Focus on getting product-market fit," Schultz advised. "If you don't have a great product, there's no point in executing more on growing it because it won't grow."

> "[The] number one problem I've seen for startups is they don't actually have product-market fit when they think they do."

WHAT DOES GOOD RETENTION LOOK LIKE?

Schultz said he gets annoyed when people ask him this question because it's so easy to figure out good retention by using dimensional reasoning.

He shared the story of Geoffrey Taylor, a British physicist who won the Nobel Prize. Just by looking at pictures of the atomic bomb, he figured out the power of the U.S. bomb.

To do it, Taylor used dimensional reasoning to figure out the power of the U.S. bomb, as well as the ratio of power between the Russian and American bombs. He ended up revealing one of the top secrets that existed in the world at that time.

Dimensional reasoning involves looking at the dimensions that are involved in a problem to come to a solution. Figuring out the ratio of power between the Russian and U.S. atomic bombs is hard. Figuring out Facebook's retention rate is not so hard.

There are approximately 2 billion people on the Internet (excluding China, where Facebook is banned), and Facebook has around 1.3 billion active users. Divide the second number by the first to find out Facebook's retention rate. It won't give you the most accurate answer, but it'll be close enough.

YOUR RETENTION RATE DEPENDS ON YOUR VERTICAL

Different verticals need different terminal retention rates for them to have successful businesses, according to Schultz.

"If you're in ecommerce, and your monthly active basis retention is close to 20%-30% of your users, you're going to do very well," he explained. "If you're on social media, and the first batch of people signing up to your product are not 80% retained, you're not going to have a massive social media site."

192

Ask yourself: Who out there is comparable? And am I anywhere close to what real success looks like in this vertical?

But, at the end of the day, no matter what vertical you're in, "retention comes from having a great idea, a great product to back up that idea, and great product-market fit," said Schultz.

OPERATING FOR GROWTH

Schultz said that startups shouldn't have growth teams because the entire company should be focused on growth. The head of growth should be the CEO, acting as the North Star for where the company wants to go.

For example, Mark Zuckerberg is Facebook's North Star because he's always been focused on growth. In the early years of Facebook, many companies focused on their registered users. But Zuckerberg focused on monthly active users instead.

Schultz explained that, when Zuckerberg talked about growth, he meant "everyone active on Facebook, not everyone signed up on Facebook" and that was the internal goal.

"It was the number he made the whole world hold Facebook to as a number that we cared about."

Airbnb followed a similar model when it came to measuring growth. They've always benchmarked themselves against the number of nights booked compared to the largest hotel chains in the world.

The take-away is that the metric for growth varies from company to company. What matters is that the CEO is focused on that metric, acting as the company's North Star.

"Let's say you have awesome product-market fit. You've built an ecommerce site, and you have 60% of people coming back every single month and making a purchase from you, which would be absolutely fantastic. How do you then take that and say, 'Now it's time to scale.'? That's where growth teams come in," Schultz said.

THE IMPORTANCE OF THE MAGIC MOMENT

For a startup, the magic moment comes when users first see value in your business. It's not nearly as romantic as the 1960s song from The Drifters, but it's a big deal.

What was the magic moment for Facebook?

Schultz said the magic moment was when you first see that first picture of one of your friends on Facebook and you realize, "Oh my god, this is what this site is about!" For Zuckerberg, that depended on getting people to 10 friends in 14 days.

The most important thing in a social media site is connecting to your friends. Without that, you have a completely empty newsfeed and you're not going to come back because you'll never get any friends telling you about things you're missing on the site.

Facebook, Twitter, WhatsApp, LinkedIn – they all pay attention to showing you the people you want to follow, connect to, and send messages to, as quickly as possible, because that's what matters.

Looking at a different vertical, eBay's magic moment is when you list an item on their platform and get paid.

You need to think about what the magic moment is for your product and get users connected to it as fast as possible. Then you can move up where that line on the retention curve graph becomes asymptotic.

Schultz said that if you can connect people with what draws them to your site, then you can go from 60% retention to 70% retention easily.

You get to that magic moment by "focusing on the marginal user – the one person who doesn't get a notification in a given day, month, or year." Building an awesome product is all about the power user, but when it comes to driving growth, you don't need to worry about people who are already using your product.

TACTICS FOR VIRALITY

According to Schultz, Sean Parker (Napster co-founder and

former Facebook president) approaches virality in terms of three things:

1. **Payload** (how many people you can hit with any given viral blast)
2. **Conversion rate**
3. **Frequency**

These three factors give you a fundamental idea of how viral a product is.

LEARNING FROM HOTMAIL

Hotmail (which later became Outlook) is "the canonical example of brilliant viral marketing," said Schultz.

When Hotmail first entered the email scene, people couldn't get free email clients because they had to be tied to their Internet Service Provider (ISP). Hotmail and a few other companies launched, and their users were able to access their mail from wherever they were.

Most of these email companies tried to get clients by spending tons of money on TV, billboard, and newspaper campaigns, but Hotmail couldn't do that because they didn't have a lot of funding. So they added a little link at the bottom of every email that said, "Sent from Hotmail. Get your free email here."

Because Hotmail users were usually emailing just one person at a time, the payload was low. But the frequency was high because users were emailing the same people over and over. So those people were going to be hit one to three times per day, increasing impressions. And the conversion rate was also really high because people didn't like being tied to their ISP email.

In the end, Hotmail became extremely viral because of its high frequency and high conversion rates.

THE TAKE-AWAY

Know what good retention looks like for your particular business. From there, growth should be the focus of everyone on your startup team.

P.S. If you're interested in learning more about viral marketing and advertising, Schultz recommends reading *Viral Loop* by Adam Penenberg and *Ogilvy on Advertising* by David Ogilvy.

PART VIII

Parting Words

Most startup advice tends to focus on the earliest stages. But once you build a successful *product*, you and your co-founders must shift your attention to building a successful *company*.

22

What Comes After Finding Product-Market Fit

Featuring: Sam Altman

Have you achieved product-market fit? If so, congratulations! Now here are the really important things that you'll need to focus on in the next stage of your startup.

In the beginning, it seems like everything you do leads up to launching. And after that, it may seem like it's all building to product–market fit. But the thing is, if your company is truly innovative and ambitious, you'll never run out of big benchmarks. That's the exciting part!

As you grow and begin to gain your footing, though, you'll

need more people. In a lecture at Stanford University, Sam Altman explained that this is the beginning of the biggest change your company will go through.

Once you start to hit 20-25 employees and have found product-market fit, "Your main job shifts from building a great product to building a great company, and it stays there for the rest of your time. This is probably the biggest shift in being a founder."

MANAGEMENT

When you're just powering through the first 12-24 months of your company, it's fine if everyone reports to the founder. But once you get an office and your company starts to expand to multiple, distinct departments, you're going to have to create a new management structure. The good news is that the best ones are simple.

First, you need to hire some senior executives. Altman said that founders often think it's too early to do this, but when they finally do it, they wish they had done so sooner.

With executives in senior positions, you have people with more experience to take the reins in areas where you and your team may not be extremely proficient. Also, they become the people that employees report to instead of you.

Altman said, "All you need is for every employee to know who their manager is and for everyone to have exactly one manager. Every manager should know their direct reports."

With this simple system in place, there should be enough clarity to avoid any confusion.

Also, as you hire more employees, it becomes even more important to have your mission clearly stated. Altman said it's as simple as writing down how and why you do things so new hires know your company values from the get-go. As he put it:

"You, as the founder, get to basically write the law."

Altman has encountered several "failure cases" to avoid as your company shifts to a new management system for more employees:

BEING AFRAID TO HIRE SENIOR PEOPLE

As the company scales, you're going to need senior execs, as opposed to the beginning stages where experience doesn't matter as much. Don't wait too long to hire because when you start to need them, you'll *really* need them.

GOING INTO "HERO MODE"

Founders can have a habit of what Altman calls "extreme leading by example." This can lead you to take over jobs you should be delegating.

If you get stuck in "Hero Mode," Altman said to let things fall behind a little while you look for a new hire. Don't stay in this mode until you burn out.

BAD DELEGATION

This kind of goes back to Hero Mode. Your leadership style should not be to ask someone to do research and then come back to you with information on which you base the final decision.

"That's how most founders delegate," said Altman. "That does not make people feel good and it certainly doesn't scale." Ask people to make decisions themselves and trust them.

NOT DEVELOPING A PERSONAL PRODUCTIVITY SYSTEM

The early stages of your startup are the prime time to start deciding the best way for you to work, personally. You need to make sure you're keeping your priorities in check while also keeping tabs on the work of your employees.

COMPANY PRODUCTIVITY

In the early days of your startup, Altman said you don't need to make an effort to focus on productivity because small teams are naturally more productive. But as your team grows, this will become a priority.

"The reason companies become unproductive is people are either not on the same page …. Or they're actively working against each other, which is obviously worse."

So, in addition to ensuring that everyone is clear on the

company's values — as written up by you, the founder — you need to provide a roadmap.

Altman said that, when you ask employees what the company's top three goals are right now, they should all have the same answer. Unfortunately this isn't usually the case.

To keep up momentum, Altman said that a big focus of your productivity has to be product, not process. That should be the core of your meetings, which you should be having with your management team once a week, plus all-hands meetings once a month.

"The goal in all of this productivity planning is that you're trying to build a company that creates a lot of value over a long period of time. And the long period of time is what's important here," he explained.

That's the hardest part of building a company. Altman said that repeat innovation will be the most difficult but most crucial part in creating a sustainable and ongoing business model that exceeds the startup phase and has staying power.

MARKETING AND PR

If there's one thing we've made clear about marketing in this book, it's that PR won't save your startup. But, while press shouldn't be one of your top priorities as an early-stage founder, as you begin to grow it should start to become something you put some effort into.

The first thing to do is decide on your key messaging, yourself. Like the company values, you want to have control over this so that your company is being talked about in the way you want.

Altman said to keep in mind, "It's very hard to change [your key messaging] once the press decides how they're going to talk about you."

He even suggested avoiding hiring a PR firm because it's better for both you and journalists if you develop a direct personal relationship rather than dealing with a middle man.

HUMAN RESOURCES

Altman said that, when people think of Human Resources, they usually think of the cheesy, overbearing characters they see on TV. But in real life, this position can be a huge asset for your team and allow you to speed up your performance.

One way this happens is with simple and frequent feedback for employees. This is also a good way to monitor for burnout. Burnout is not good for employees or your company, so make sure you've turned the workflow from sprint to marathon mode.

With compensation, Altman suggested maintaining bands tied to performance. For example, keeping all of your mid-level employees around the same range will avoid problems in the future and keep things fair. He said that another thing to take into account when thinking about human resources is to be generous with equity.

"You should think about [the fact that] for the next 10 years, you're going to be giving out 3-5 percent of the company every year because you just get bigger and bigger," he said. "So the individual grants gets smaller but in actuality it's a lot of stock … If you value your people, you should be doing this."

HIRING

Altman suggested hiring an actual recruiter because, at a time when you'll be growing so quickly, hiring can take a lot of your own time that could be spent on building the business.

He also said to make sure you hire with diversity in mind, primarily diversity of experiences. While it's good to hire people with an outlook that aligns with your vision, different perspectives can make for a more dynamic, indispensable team.

Note that your hiring process may cause other early employees to be uprooted or to expect a promotion to the head of their department. Altman said to avoid this if it's at the expense of finding someone else who is more experienced.

He also explained that it's important to sit down with those early employees and talk with them about where they see their future at the company and decide on what you can both do to navigate that.

LEGAL, FINANCE, AND ACCOUNTING

During the time that all of your legal documents can be easily sorted and contained, get them organized. If you wait to do that until you start growing, you'll end up in a real bind with potentially costly repercussions.

Here are some especially important things to take care of in the world of paperwork.

(Again, this advice is primarily directed at startups founded in the United States but also covers some topics like allocating stock to employees that will be useful to entrepreneurs around the globe.)

STOCKS

Altman said to remember this around the time of series B funding:

"Most founders don't actually want to sell stock until the company is worth like a billion dollars ... You can actually safely set this up after things start working in the next financing round and then you can sell it two, three, four years down the road."

PATENTS

To ensure that all of your patent ducks are in a row, Altman said that, in the U.S., you have 12 months after you announce something to grab a patent on it. So, 11 months after you've spoken publicly about your idea, get a provisional patent that will basically start that process.

He also reminds founders to file trademarks for U.S. and major international markets and get all the domains for your business.

FINANCIAL PLANNING AND ANALYSIS

Altman said this is a good time to get a jump on your financial planning and analysis. This is a hire that people usually think about way too late in the game.

"You almost certainly get better results [if you hire a full-time fundraiser] than if you hire an investment banker or someone else," he said. "And you end up paying way less money and take literally half the dilution."

Whether it's you who's fundraising or someone you've hired, he said it's important to be clear and direct about asking for what you want.

TAX STRUCTURING

There is a way to structure your taxes by assigning your IP to a certain corporation overseas that licenses it back to the U.S. and this spares you corporate tax.

Altman said to dig a little deeper with more research on this. But it can put you on the same level as your competition, which is likely doing the same thing.

YOUR MENTAL HEALTH

If you aren't able to keep it together then, no matter how hard you work, all of this advice means nothing.

As he mentioned before, Altman said **it's important that you consciously make the mental switch from a 24/7 sprint to a more well-paced marathon.** This will keep your enthusiasm high and help you avoid mistakes.

As your company gets bigger and you get more exposure, it's inevitable that people will go from loving to hating you, so you're going to have to be ready to handle that emotionally.

He said that, in order to keep a clear head, you have to remember to take vacations. Otherwise, if you lose your focus, you'll flee to easier self-gratifying tasks that aren't moving your business forward.

If you get especially drained, acquisition may look like more of an appealing option. He said that this mindset will put you at a major disadvantage against your competitors who are in it for the long haul.

"[Entertaining acquisition conversations] is one of the biggest killers of companies ... You distract yourself. You get demoralized if it doesn't happen. If an offer does come in, it's really low. You've already mentally thought that you're done and so you take the offer. As a general rule, don't start any acquisition conversation unless you're willing to sell for a pretty low number."

Losing a grip on your own psychology is something that Altman said can kill companies quickly and easily. But, if you handle your mental state in a way that's healthy, intentional, and positive, he said, "You'll be in a far, far better place."

THE TAKE-AWAY

The planning doesn't stop once you're on your way to a swanky new office and hiring big name people to join your team. In fact, that's when the planning stakes get even higher.

In the long run, making the transition to actually building your business will be even more important than your initial launch.

Afterword

Thank you for reading *How to Start a Startup!*

As we mentioned at the outset, our hope is that this book will take the wisdom and energy of Silicon Valley and spread it worldwide, motivating and educating aspiring entrepreneurs in the Valley, throughout the United States, and around the globe.

We would be honored to stay in touch with you throughout your entrepreneurial journey. Please let us know how the advice contained in this book has helped you, share other feedback, or reach out with any questions at **startupbook@thinkapps.com**.

ThinkApps believes in the power of software products. Today these come in the form of mobile, web, Internet of Things (IoT), and virtual reality apps, but the medium is constantly evolving. To learn more about the

products and services offered by ThinkApps, you can visit
http://thinkapps.com.

tech co's are like organisms
sustenance fr sales/revenue
must imitate/innovate to survive/thrive
those that fail to adapt starve to death
only long-term security comes fr
the innovation that is difficult to
imitate (will eventually be
imitated (rev eng'd) or (stolen)
however)
expenses are like burned cals also
"only the paranoid survive"
ie organism: E::tech co: $

Made in United States
North Haven, CT
03 May 2022